Direct Mail is Alive and Kickin'

Jeff Charlton

Direct Mail is Alive and Kickin'

© 2015 by Jeff Charlton

ISBN: 978-1-63110-146-5

Printed in the United States of America by
Independent Publishing Corporation
Chesterfield, Missouri 63005

*This book is dedicated
to every business owner
who has struggled for years
to find a marketing solution
that consistently delivers
steady and increasing profits.*

Contents

Despite the growth of the Internet,

Direct Mail is as powerful as ever – and growing.

Learn how to combine

the power of Direct Mail Marketing with

the power of the Internet

to supercharge your results

and get more qualified leads

than ever before.

INTRODUCTION

This book is primarily about marketing in general, with an emphasis on Direct Mail Marketing. Before I get into the nitty-gritty, I want to spend a little bit of time telling you my story, and how I'm uniquely qualified to educate you in this field. I hope you enjoy it.

My Story

At the time of this writing, I am 52 years old. I have been a salesman and marketer since I was an 11 year old Boy Scout. It took me about 15 years, until after I had graduated from college and was several years into my career, to realize exactly what I was doing. Turns out I was a salesman and Direct Response Marketer. Once I realized it, I embraced it and have been a student and practitioner of Direct Response Marketing ever since. So let's start at the beginning.

It all started back when I was eleven years old and joined the local Boy Scout troop. Back in those days, we lived in a lower, middle-class neighborhood, and no one had much money, so we had fundraising projects to pay for various camping trips and activities.

Our big fundraiser every year was selling fertilizer. That's right—fertilizer! Not cookies, not candy, but fertilizer. Our scoutmaster realized we could earn as much money selling fertilizer as we could selling five other items.

You can imagine, at eleven years old, I had no idea how to sell fertilizer. But it was a simple sale. We had one kind of fertilizer, 13 – 13 – 13, and one price. I went door-to-door asking people if they wanted to buy some fertilizer. My goal was to sell 40 bags, which would raise enough money to pay for my summer camp. The troop had a prize for the guy who sold the most, and I wanted to be that guy. My best friend Dave was also in the troop, and he and I had a friendly competition going to see who could win the prize.

That first year, Dave and I both met our goal of 40 bags (free summer camp), but neither won the prize for the most sales in the troop. That irritated me, so I thought about how I could win the prize the next year. I came up with a plan to create a simple flyer, and pass it out in the neighborhood in advance of the fertilizer sale. Since I didn't have to wait for people to answer the door, I could cover a whole lot of ground a lot faster by passing out flyers. (I learned this technique from Dave's dad, who used to have us hand out flyers for his pharmacy.)

I didn't realize back then that I was essentially using Direct Mail to get out a marketing message. Granted, my message was pretty straightforward and simple, but I did put an offer in front of people. I even sweetened the pot a little. I knew that most yards required more than one bag, so I got the troop leader to agree that if I could sell multiple bags to the same person, I could give them a discount.

The prices listed on the flyer were one bag for $10, three bags for $25, and six bags for $50. I put my phone number on the flyer asked people to call me if they were interested. In addition, the flyer mentioned that if they wanted this special blend, they would have to be one of the first to get it before it ran out.

The truth is, we really did have a special blend. 13 – 13 – 13 fertilizer was not sold in stores. It was a special blend, only used commercially, that worked much better than fertilizer sold in stores. People who used it absolutely loved it.

I even added a couple of testimonials to our flyer. I had happy customers from previous years' sales, so I used their names to help promote the product. The flyer was handwritten, and my Dad took it to his office to make about 300 copies. I also wrote, in red, a handwritten comment to all the people who had bought from me the previous year.

I had several flyer recipients call me and place their order over the phone. I asked them if they knew anyone else that might want to order as well. Several of the people ordered enough for other family members, or referred friends.

I sold more than my 40 bag allotment from the initial phone calls. Once our troop officially opened up sales, and we were allowed to go door-to-door, I easily won the award for the most sales. I went to all the streets that had people who already had ordered, and dropped their names when knocking on the doors of the neighbors. In fact, I sold three times more than the next closest guy (even Dave, although he also did very well.) There were so many sales, they had to deliver the fertilizer on a tractor-trailer, completely loaded. More than 50% of the sales were from Dave and me.

Not only did I use Direct Response Marketing, but I had created an irresistible offer, testimonials, scarcity, and a deadline. These are basic principles discussed in this book that are critical to success in direct marketing.

Fast-Forward To The Age Of 14.

I was still in Boy Scouts, but I had begun cutting lawns in the neighborhood. One day, one of my customers asked me if I would paint his house. I'd never done that before, but it seemed simple enough so I said yes. He agreed to pay me four dollars per hour. At the time I was earning five dollars for each lawn I cut. Minimum wage was $1.75 per hour back then, so $4 seemed like a ton of cash.

I earned $200 from that first house I painted, which seemed like a massive amount of money, compared to what I was making in the lawn business. I did a good job on the house, and the guy agreed to allow me to use his name as a referral. I remembered the success I had with the flyer to sell fertilizer, so I used the same technique for selling house painting jobs. I received a couple of phone calls from my initial flyer distribution in my neighborhood. I then went to other neighbors, knocked on their doors and asked them if they wanted their house painted. I mentioned the happy customer I had, and amazingly, two other neighbors agreed to allow me to paint their houses. Given I was working alone, that was enough to keep me busy most of the summer.

Over the winter, all I could think about was how I could expand my budding business. I enlisted the help of my best friend Eddie, whose uncle was in the painting business. Eddie had never painted houses either, but since his uncle was in the business somehow that made him an expert. (And we used that fact to help build us up as experts.)

That second year, the only marketing materials we had were a flyer with our names and phone numbers, and the three references from the previous summer.

On spring break instead of playing baseball like our other friends, we used the same technique we used for the fertilizer sales. We delivered flyers to every house in our neighborhood and a couple of surrounding neighborhoods. We also went door-to-door, asking owners if they wanted their house painted.

We painted about six houses that summer. As I think back, what really made us effective in our marketing efforts was that we had referrals, and we could point to their houses because they were in the same neighborhood. The flyer approach worked because it allowed us to put our names in front of people even if they didn't answer the door.

Again, I didn't realize it, but I was using Direct Response Marketing.

At the time we were too young to drive, so we hauled the ladders and equipment down the street. Each of us was holding one end of a 24-foot ladder, with drop-cloths and buckets hanging from the ladder. It was quite a sight. We lugged the stuff from one end of the subdivision to the other, which was about a mile away. It didn't matter to us; we were making money.

Back then there was no Internet and no voicemail. Our strategy was a simple handwritten flyer, a knock on the door and a personal sales call. We didn't have any smooth sales presentation. It was as simple as asking, "Hey, do you want us to paint your house? We did Joe Smith's and Bob Jones' house last year." But it worked. As I look back, I'm amazed that anyone would let a 14 or 15-year-old kid paint their house. But I think they were impressed that someone of that age had the ambition to even attempt such a feat. We had testimonials from happy customers that would vouch for the fact that we could do the work and do it well. Besides, our prices were much cheaper than union painters'. (I'm sure the union guys were not too happy about that, but no one ever picketed our jobs so I guess we were lucky.)

The next summer I had my driver's license, and decided to expand the business even more. We had some business cards printed, and we upgraded to typewritten flyers on colored paper. We didn't have the money for Direct Mail, so we continued to deliver the flyers on foot (actually on our bikes because we could cover more ground in less time.) We stapled a business card to a flyer, rolled it up with a rubber band, and as we rode by on our bikes, we slipped it over the knob on the mailbox. We printed and distributed about 1,000 flyers over a couple days during spring break.

We got a handful of phone calls from that initial campaign. We went to see those people in person, then canvassed the surrounding houses on foot. When we spoke to the people in the surrounding houses, we told them their neighbor had just contracted with us to do a paint job. It was amazing how easy it was to sell someone when they knew that someone else had already said yes. This was also a form of referral marketing, even though we hadn't even done the jobs yet, in this case. We still had our testimonials from previous years, but we found it equally as effective to tell someone their next-door neighbor just said yes.

We also invested in a yard sign to place in the yard of the house we were painting. Once we finished a house, we asked the owner if they knew anyone else who might want their house painted. Almost every one of them would give us at least one name.

We booked about 5 jobs on spring break, before the summer. Once we started painting in the summer, we never had to knock on another door. We had more jobs than we could keep up with due to the referral system we had in place.

That is where I learned a lesson in supply and demand. As we became busier and busier, I began to raise prices as the demand increased. Amazingly, no matter how much I raised the price, no one ever turned me down. By the time I was a senior in college, I had a painting van, and 11 of my closest friends working for me. We even subcontracted jobs to four of my high school coaches, who also painted houses in the summer, but had a hard time finding jobs.

Our Direct Response system was so successful, we never had to do anything different. We invested a few days over spring break each year to get sales going for that summer, and the rest took care of itself. Every year we had to turn people down because we just could not do all the jobs.

Fast-Forward A Few Years.

After graduating from college with a degree in civil engineering, I went to work for Procter & Gamble as an industrial engineer. (By the way, my parents could not afford to pay for college, which was what motivated me to be so aggressive in my painting business. I wanted to be able to pay my own way through college.)

I quickly learned I was not cut out to work in corporate America, nor was I cut out to work in a manufacturing plant. I was a salesman and entrepreneur at heart, and I knew I needed to get into business for myself again. But the funny thing is, when I first took the job as an engineer, I didn't see myself as a salesman or marketer. I honestly thought that what I had done as a kid was no big deal, and that sales and marketing were things I wanted no part of.

After I had worked as an engineer and seen the reality of corporate America, I totally changed my tune. The light bulb went on and I realized that I should be an entrepreneur. I had to accept that I needed to learn sales and marketing, as they are vital elements to success.

I didn't know it at the time, but the lessons I learned in the painting business laid the groundwork for my future career.

Once I realized engineering was not my future, I started looking for an opportunity to get back into my own business. I found an opportunity to work for a small printing company as a salesman. Even though I didn't know anything about printing, it seemed like an interesting business. I made a deal with the owner that I would come to work for him, learn the business, learn how to sell, and take over the company when he retired in five years. I saw the path to have my own business again, and working for him for a few years would allow me to learn the business, and learn how to be a salesman.

At the time, I didn't realize I had any sales experience. Even though I had done door-to-door sales for the last eight years in my painting company, to me, that didn't even count. (It turns out, that was great training.)

My new boss told me the secret to success was cold calls. Trusting that he was the expert, I gave it 110% effort. I pounded the streets and phones every available moment during the day. On nights and weekends, I read everything I possibly could about printing, marketing, and sales. I wanted to be the most knowledgeable guy in my market. I suppose that was the engineer coming through in me. I felt that I had to be an expert to be confident in front of a customer. It didn't take me long to become an expert, and I fairly quickly built a good book of business. In fact I went from zero to $1,000,000 in annual sales in two and a half years.

One thing I learned during that process was that door-to-door cold calls, although effective, were inefficient. So instead, I chose to make my cold calls on the phone. I figured I could make three to five times as many phone calls as I could in-person calls, thus dramatically increasing my effectiveness. My boss was hesitant to allow me to do this, because he had been brought up pounding the streets. But my results proved I was right.

In those days, voicemail was in its infancy stages. Email was nonexistent. The fax machine was the most modern method of electronic communication.

Although I was successful with that company, I was not completely happy with the direction the owner was going, and felt I could do it better myself. So after two and half years, I abandoned the idea of buying his company, and resigned.

Even though I had been successful working for the small printing company as a salesman, I was recently divorced and left with no money. I was starting all over again, in my basement, from square one. It was even harder this time, because I had a sales contract that prevented me from calling on any customers or contacts I developed in the last two and half years. I couldn't talk to anybody that I had contacted about business, including my friends.

My entire investment in the new business consisted of a $30 table from Walmart, a chair, phone, cardboard file cabinet, and a $600 computer. Since I had already proven that I could sell, and I knew how to do cold calls, I started pounding the phones again. I remember spending eight hours a day in my basement, making cold calls on the phone. There were days when I didn't get a single appointment. It was grueling. But since I had proven before I could do it, I plowed forward.

In order to increase my chances of success, I added an element of Direct Mail to the formula. I would make the initial call, find out the correct contact information and address, then send a cover letter with a business card through the mail to the prospect. I would then follow up with a phone call introducing myself and requesting an appointment. After I landed a customer, I sent a series of mail pieces to them just to remind them I was around. It was nothing fancy, mostly just typed and personally signed letters. But the addition of Direct Mail increased my results dramatically, and I was able to repeat my success of zero to $1 million in less than two years.

I used that very simple system for several years. About five years into the business, I had become pretty skilled in writing effective Direct Mail pieces. That is when I decided to branch off into the information products business, and develop my own marketing system. I sold that marketing system using a series of Direct Mail sales letters. I had a frontend of $40, and a backend of $1,000.

My first test was a 5,000 piece sales letter that garnered a 3% response. Back then I was a print broker, which meant I didn't have any printing presses. I contracted all printing through other local print shops. My cost was about $.60 per letter, or $3,000 in total cost for 5,000 pieces. My initial mailing generated about $6,000 in sales.

I was flabbergasted. I thought I'd won the lottery. That $6,000 was just the beginning. I now had 150 customers that I could market my backend product to. My mailings quickly expanded from 5,000 pieces to 150,000 pieces every month.

It was not all wine and roses; I did make a few mistakes along the way. The biggest mistake I made was getting cocky with my initial success. Instead of being conservative and testing new offers, I started a couple new programs and mailed 50,000 pieces with the first mailing. Unfortunately, that mailing didn't do as well as my initial offer, and I lost money. The good news is I learned my lesson quickly, and didn't repeat that mistake. I never do anything new without a test first. Even if we have a successful test, we do not immediately ramp up but do it in a slow and controlled manner. That way we can tweak and adjust along the way before risking too much money.

Fast-Forward To Today

My company has grown to the point that we have a full manufacturing plant that produces printed products, direct mail, self-published books, (we printed this book), promotional products, and embroidered apparel. We help business owners develop marketing programs utilizing Direct Mail and Direct Response Marketing to provide a steady stream of qualified leads for their business. All businesses need more leads and more customers to make more money. We realize that if we help business owners make more money, we will benefit at the same time.

We're not a huge company; we have about 40 employees. We operate with old-fashioned Midwestern values. We are honest, we work hard, and we do what we say we are going to do 100% of the time. One of my biggest pet peeves is computerized phone answering systems. In my company, during normal business hours, we always answer the phone with one of our local staff members. They will always answer with a smile on their face and bend over backwards to help the client. We use technology where it makes sense, but there are some things good old-fashioned human relations can't beat.

I tell you all this because I want you to understand that this is not rocket science. I never took a single class in English in college. I'm a technical guy at heart with an engineering degree. I grew up in a middle-class family with old-fashioned Midwestern values. Hard work has always been important to me.

I was lucky that I sort of naturally had some entrepreneurial instincts at a young age. But it wasn't until after I worked as an engineer that I realized being an expert at marketing and copywriting was important to success in my business. I made it my mission to learn how to be an effective marketer and copywriter.

Just like I studied printing and salesmanship when I first got into the printing business, I have that same appetite for marketing these days. I am constantly buying new programs, attending seminars, and studying the craft. If you think you know it all, you're in trouble. There's always something new to learn and the world is always changing. You have to change with the times and keep up with the latest techniques and systems.

I wrote this book to give you a general overview of marketing in general, and specifically an education in Direct Response Marketing. I chose the title *Direct Mail is Alive and Kickin'* because the perception is that the Internet has taken over everything, and old-fashioned Direct Mail Marketing is no longer effective.

That could not be further from the truth, and statistics prove it.

When you're done reading, hopefully you will see that the most effective marketing programs combine both online and offline strategies. I hope you enjoy this book, and are motivated to become a marketing expert yourself. If you're interested, we can help you create an effective program for your own business.

Jeff Charlton

I Thought Direct Mail was Dead!

How many times have you heard "Direct Mail is dead?" Every time the post office raises rates, fewer people mail. Many people have the mistaken impression that increased postal rates make Direct Mail unaffordable.

We've all been taught that online advertising and email marketing is the key to millions. "That old-fashioned mail stuff is for old folks." There are online gurus making a fortune everywhere. The allure of Online Marketing is exciting. Sending out a few emails and watching the money flow in is a concept that attracts many.

Some of that is true. However, if Direct Mail is dead, why do we see almost every major online retailer spending millions of dollars on all types of media, including Direct Mail?

They're doing it because Direct Mail works. It works in just about every industry, but some better than others. They're also doing it because they know a mixed approach is more effective than one single approach by itself.

What happened to make Direct Mail appealing again?

I'm sure you can relate to getting hundreds, if not thousands of daily emails, most of which are unsolicited. Even the emails you agreed to receive are overwhelming. You have spam filters, but they don't catch it all. Half the time your spam filter catches a few emails that you want, so you end up having to search through the spam filter to find the good emails, which frustrates you more.

It seems like every time you buy something online, you end up with emails from at least 10 different companies. You start deleting as fast as you can. Often, legitimate offers that you might actually have an interest in get deleted.

There is no question that when email first got popular, and Google AdWords was still new, there was a window of opportunity during which you could focus strictly online and make a bucket of cash.

It is still possible, but it is getting more difficult every day. Plus, there are a lot of businesses that just don't work well online. Retail, restaurants, and service businesses have a tough time marketing strictly online.

To make matters worse, just when you think you have an online system figured out, the technology changes. Google often changes the rules, or a million other factors out of your control change, and it's back to the drawing board to come up with another strategy. Email for business purposes is no longer free. Most auto-responder services charge fees that go up as you get more people on your list.

Pay-per-click advertising continues to get more expensive. It is not unusual to pay $10 per click or more for one key word. The cost of advertising online has skyrocketed, which makes earning a profit that much more difficult. It certainly has made it more complicated and risky.

Do you honestly look at every email in your inbox? Chances are you don't even look at one percent of them. You definitely don't look at those that come unsolicited.

To make it even more difficult, the legal system has stiff penalties for those who abuse email, and it is very easy to find yourself in an expensive legal battle when all you're trying to do is innocently promote your business.

Let's take a look at Direct Mail in contrast to Online Marketing.

First, there are no laws against sending unsolicited mail to someone's physical mailbox. No one is damaged and it doesn't cost them a dime to receive mail. It is true that some people get irritated by what is commonly known as "junk" mail. But it is not illegal, and you will not get in trouble sending it.

Secondly, even the busiest person eventually has to go to the mailbox, pick up the mail, and shuffle through it to decide what to keep and what to throw away. Okay, some of the busiest people don't look at their mail; they have someone else do it. But that doesn't mean you can't get their attention using mail.

You have at least a second or two to get their attention. It is very easy to delete an email without ever seeing a single word in the email. It is not so easy to get rid of a Direct Mail piece without at least taking a quick glance at it.

Third, most of us spend a good part of our day staring at the computer screen. There is still a large part of society that enjoys reading the printed word on paper. I rarely will read any sort of long document on the Internet, but I will take a long letter, or report, or a book, and read it in my easy chair.

Let me give you a few facts to chew on.

- The Direct Marketing Association says that 73% of people prefer to receive a Direct Mail solicitation vs. an email solicitation.

- 50% of consumers say they pay more attention to postal mail than email
  (Epsilon Preference Study, 2011).

- 60% of consumers say they enjoy checking their mailbox and receiving mail
  (Epsilon Preference Study, 2011).

- 65% of consumers say they receive too many emails every day.

- A fast-growing percentage of people express frustration and resentment with email marketing even from sources with which they have a good relationship
  (Alliance Research).

- The preference for Direct Mail even extends to the 18 to 34 age group
  (Epsilon Preference Study, 2011).

- "Tangible materials such as Direct Mail trigger a much deeper level of emotional processing than any other media. They also generate more activity in the area of brain associated with integration of visual and facial information". This basically means Direct Mail has a better chance than any other media of motivating a person to take action.

  ("Using Neuroscience to Understand the Role of Direct Mail," a study by Bangor University and Millward Brown)

- 98% of consumers retrieve their mail from the mailbox the day it is delivered and 77% sort through it the same day

  (USPS data, reported in DM news 2/11).

These statistics prove Direct Mail is not dead.

Not only is it not dead, but it is arguably more effective at creating an emotional connection with potential clients.

Many marketers are starting to use Direct Mail to drive people online. They are also doing the reverse—gathering leads using online methods, then using Direct Mail to close the deal. The sooner you can get people from your online system offline, the more effective your overall marketing system will be.

An ideal strategy is to use both Direct Mail and Online Marketing as a tag-team approach.

Direct Mail is especially effective in the real estate industry. Whether you are a real estate investor or agent, finding the email addresses of potential homeowners who want to sell their house is extremely difficult. Even if you can find email addresses, targeting them to specific neighborhoods is also difficult.

Contrast that with Direct Mail. You can rent a very targeted list, in a specific location, with specific demographics about the home, the value of the house, whether it has a mortgage, whether the mortgage is paid on time, the equity in the house, absentee owners, and a host of other factors. (Note: When you "rent" a list, you are paying a fee to the list owner for the rights to mail to that list for a specified number of times.)

Both agents and investors can pick specific properties to target based on their own personal business criteria, and send them personalized Direct Mail pieces that speak directly to the owner and the terms they want them to hear.

Direct-mail also works great for any business that can easily identify their target prospect. The more narrow your list of ideal prospects, the better Direct Mail can be. The reason for this is if you really know who your target prospect is, and what they want, you can craft a specific Direct Mail message to speak to those needs. Contrast this with something like a radio advertisement, which is heard by anyone who is listening that radio station. Yes it goes to a wide audience, but it is very difficult to deal with specific needs of a specific audience using that type of media.

Plus, if your target audience is a manageable number, you can afford to spend a lot for very extensive Direct Mail packages, with multiple touches, which can really be effective in getting the prospect's attention.

Direct Mail *is* alive and well.

I thought email and web advertising were cheaper.

Since anyone can send a single email basically free of charge, the perception is that email marketing is much cheaper than Direct Mail Marketing. On the surface, that is true. But let's dig a little deeper.

First of all, as I said earlier, sending single emails through your own email account is free in most cases. However, most marketing systems utilize an auto-responder, and those systems are not free. The more emails you send, the more it costs. Often, you'll need more than one auto-responder system to manage various campaigns. Different systems have different pros and cons, and the more sophisticated you get in your marketing, the more difficult it becomes to find one that can do it all for you.

Second, renting a targeted email list is far more expensive than renting a targeted mailing list. Even if you can find an email list to rent, which is hit and miss at best, the email addresses change constantly, and deliverability is extremely low. The only way to email a cold list is to find a paid service willing to take the legal risk. These services are often very expensive. Plus, the recipients are not very receptive for all the aforementioned reasons.

If you don't buy an email list, you have to get a lead some other way, online. Yes, organic search is possible. If you don't know what organic search means, I am talking about going to Google or Yahoo and searching for a given topic. Organic are the results that come up, usually around the middle of the page, just below the paid ads. Organic search is free, but getting noticed is not easy.

There are thousands of companies that will take your money and promise to help you get noticed. They call that SEO, which stands for Search Engine Optimization. It is extremely expensive and time-consuming to get any kind of results with SEO. And it does not happen overnight. It takes months, often years, to get ranked on the first page of Google for important keywords. (There is no guarantee you will ever get to the first page.)

SEO is not targeted at all. You are depending totally on chance that someone happens to find your webpage, and they happen to live in the area you are targeting, and they happen to be interested enough in your product or service to opt in to your webpage.

Once they opt in to your webpage, you have permission to market to them via email or other means. But the chance of all that happening without you spending significant money on online advertising is slim.

There are many choices for online advertising, in all different price ranges. The most popular is pay-per-click advertising, commonly done through Google. Paying for clicks can be very expensive. These days most common search terms in just about any industry go for more than $10 per click. It doesn't take very long to spend thousands, even tens of thousands of dollars, just getting people to go to your website. And there's no guarantee that they will read anything, or opt in to your mailing list after they click. Opt-in rates can vary, depending on what you're asking the person to do. But anything over 5% is considered insanely high.

The bottom line is, even though Online Marketing seems inexpensive on the surface, by the time you add up all these various costs, it can be extremely expensive.

Online Marketing is effective after a lead has requested more information from you. At that time you're free to send all the emails you want using fairly cost-effective systems. But again, it is not free.

Direct Mail is a cost-effective way to get people's attention. Using Direct Mail to generate interested prospects, then following up with online tools can be an extremely powerful marketing system.

Let's run through some numbers

A typical Direct Mail campaign might cost you, in rough numbers, one dollar per mail piece. Let's say you mail 1,000 mail pieces and spend $1,000. Let's say you got a 2% response rate, which is 20 people responding to your offer. I am assuming in this case your offer had to do with simply responding for more information or something free.

Essentially it cost you $50 per lead. Let's also say you have an effective sales team that can close 10% of the leads. Let's say a typical sale for you could deliver a profit of at least $10,000. In this example you would close 2 leads, and profit $20,000. So you spent $1,000 and earned $20,000 in return. I would say that is a good return.

Now let's look at a typical online scenario. Let's say you decide to do a pay-per-click campaign, and wanted to get 20 leads to opt into your website. Let's also assume the typical price per click is $10. It is not unusual for an online campaign to require

20 clicks for every 1 opt-in. Using that scenario, to get 20 leads online, it would require 400 clicks, at $10 per click, or $4,000 to get the same 20 leads you got with the Direct Mail piece.

If you assume you're a much better marketer and can get one opt in for every 10 clicks, which is a 10% opt in rate, it would still take you 200 clicks to get 20 leads. At $10 per click, that is still $2,000. This is still double the cost of the Direct Mail campaign.

Of course there are other options for online advertising, and they all have different rates. But few can be as effective as Direct Mail, when you really break down the true cost of the entire campaign.

Consumers prefer "snail" mail over email

For you younger folks who never heard of "snail mail," let me explain. When email first came out, traditional postal mail was given the nickname "snail mail," mainly because it was not instantaneous like email.

Let's get back to why consumers prefer "snail" mail.

There are several reasons for this. First, it is simply easier to read something printed on paper than on the computer screen. Second, you can do things with paper and ink, such as adding scents, special papers, incredibly rich photos, and other things that create an emotional response, that you can't do on a computer screen.

Another benefit is that people can put Direct Mail aside and come back to it and read it later. I often collect my mail and save it for my next airline flight. I will go through it in more detail on the plane. Technically you can do the same thing with an email, but that is much more difficult to do given the information overload that we all face. Plus, if you get an email on your desktop at the office, unless you have a very sophisticated mobile device and understand cloud systems, it is difficult to take an email received in one place and read it later on another device. Things such as product catalogs or items that need to be presented using high quality images, such as high-end cars, just work better on paper.

I spend all day in front of the computer screen. I actually enjoy getting away from it, and reading things on good old-fashioned paper. It's actually relaxing to sit in my easy chair and read mail, magazines, catalogs, etc. I am not the only one who feels this way.

Lastly, a Direct Mail piece can be shared with other people much more easily than an email. Not that you can't send an email easily, but for all the reasons mentioned before, we all face information overload in our inbox. If you want someone's opinion on a Direct Mail piece, handing it to them and asking them to read it has a much better chance of getting their attention.

Direct Mail is Alive and Kickin'!

Chapter 2

What Business Are You In?

Now that we've established that Direct Mail still is an effective marketing tool in today's market, let's step back for a minute and talk about basic marketing.

Before you can embark on any type of marketing campaign, especially a Direct Mail Marketing campaign, you need to understand all the variables that will affect your success. That all starts with understanding your business and what you're really selling.

The single most important thing you need to understand is…

You are in the marketing business, whether you like it or not!

Let me explain.

Whether you're a carpet cleaner, plumber, doctor, lawyer, or real estate investor, you are in the marketing business. No matter how good you are at your trade, if you don't have any customers (or patients), you don't have a business. Learning how to attract and acquire customers is necessary in every business, and is the single most important criteria to success in every business.

Your product or service is important, and a vital element, but it is secondary. You can hire people to do what you do fairly easily. Doctors who have more patients than they can handle can hire more doctors. Law firms who have too many cases can hire more lawyers. Retailers can hire more clerks. Real estate firms can hire more agents. Manufacturers can make more products. All that is the easy part. (Unless you possess some skill that no one else has, and in that case you probably don't have a marketing problem. But that is not the norm.)

In almost every industry, finding someone to do the work is the easy part. But hiring a person to get you more customers is not so easy. It is far easier to find someone with a specific skill than it is to find a person who can market and sell. That particular skill is extremely hard to find.

You might think all you have to do is hire some salespeople and that will solve your problem. Ask any business owner who has tried to hire salespeople and he or she will tell you differently. The only way to be successful in hiring salespeople is to first have a marketing system in place that drives leads to the sales force. It is critical that the system works in such a way that clients or patients are attracted to you. You want them knocking on your door, wanting your product or service. That way you do not need superstar salespeople to close the deal. If your business relies on having superstar salespeople to both find and close leads, you are going to struggle to succeed.

The best person to become the marketing expert is you, the business owner—especially when the business is small. Even medium and large businesses require the people at the top to be savvy marketers. The sooner you can accept the fact that the most important thing you can do is to learn how to be an effective marketer, the sooner you'll be on the road to success greater than you've ever achieved before.

You Market Or You Die!

That may sound a bit harsh, but it is the truth of any business. Every successful business needs a steady stream of new prospects and customers coming to the door every week and month. No matter how good you are, you will lose business over time. You have to constantly be replacing those customers you lose, and if you want to grow you have to get new customers on top of that.

The days of sitting back and hoping for people to come to you are over. In this market, people have too many options, including going online for just about every product or service imaginable. I am in the printing business, and 30 years ago you could open a print shop, put a sign in the window, and people would come to you with orders. You didn't need salesmen, just a storefront.

Nowadays, most of those storefront businesses are gone. People can order their printing online, at OfficeMax, FedEx Kinko's, and even at Sam's. Many years ago, we employed a sales force to go out and find business. But that has become extremely tough as well. You used to be able hire a salesman, hand him a phone and a desk, and tell him to go sell something. No more.

It is no different for restaurants, drycleaners, insurance agencies, retail stores, and the like. To be successful in business in today's market, you must invest a percentage of your cash, each month, in a consistent and predictable marketing program. You must find ways to attract new customers and clients to come to you over your competition. You need to put a system in place where the prospects are calling you. Then you can have your salesforce talk to them and close sales. If you don't, your business will die. It's that simple.

You also have to be more creative than ever before. You need to use as many different media sources as possible to generate prospects. Because different people respond to different things, using a diverse mix of media is smart business.

What Does A Typical Marketing Plan Look Like?

You need to have two different marketing funnels. What is a marketing funnel? A marketing funnel is a series of steps that systematically draw a prospect or customer through the buying process.

You need to have a funnel for prospects, and you need to have a funnel for existing customers. You need two because you handle these two different groups of people in different ways.

With prospects, you need to introduce them to your product or service, and entice them to try you out. With existing customers, you need to stay in front of them so they don't forget you, and also to encourage them to spend more than they are already spending. Your best source of additional revenue is always your existing customers. Too many businesses ignore existing customers and spend all their marketing dollars on finding new clients.

It's ten times easier to get more from an existing customer, or reactivate a past customer who has stopped buying from you, than it is to get a new prospect to buy from you. But both funnels are very important.

Let's look at a typical Marketing Funnel for both prospects and customers.

For prospects:

Send out postcards or sales letters to a target market, enticing the prospect to either call you or go to a webpage to take advantage of a free offer.

Enroll the prospect in both a Direct Mail, and an email series of messages that continually reminds them why they should do business with you. You can do this by publishing a monthly or quarterly newsletter. You can send out postcard offers monthly. You send out regular emails, at least one a week, with special offers.

Make audio clips and videos, and direct your prospects to listen to review them both online and offline.

It is important to reach these people by mail at least once a month, and by email at least once a week. But be sure you're offering them value and not garbage. If you send them garbage it will either end up in the deleted file or in the trash can.

For customers:

For customers, many of the same rules apply, except since they've already bought from you, your offers will likely be different. But you can still use newsletters, Direct Mail postcards, sales letters, and emails to communicate with them.

Your goal should be to upsell them on additional product purchases from you. Your goal is to extend the lifetime value of each customer. A secondary goal is to make sure that they do not forget about you the next time they are ready to purchase something you sell.

Why don't people buy from you?

Marketing is simple when you boil it down.
There are five reasons people will not buy from you:

- **They don't have a need for your product.**

- **They don't have any money.**

- **They do not need your product right now.**

- **They don't trust you.**

- **They are already buying your product from someone else and are happy.**

- **Let's talk about each one of these areas.**

They don't have a need for your product.

This one is easy. People don't always need what you have to sell. If you are in the real estate business, and you approach someone who loves their house and has no intention of moving, no matter how often or how well you solicit their business, they are going to ignore you.

If you're a doctor and the person is not sick, the prospect will likely say no for now. An automotive shop might have the greatest deal in the world for brakes, but if you don't need brakes, you won't buy

But that doesn't mean they won't need it in the future sometime!

Timing is everything, but as a small business, you can't afford to market to everyone. This is where targeting the right people is so important. It is vital that you identify people who have the best chance of being interested in your product in the very near future. Those are the people you target.

Examples of people who have demonstrated that they want your products and services are:

- **Your existing customers**

- **Your competitors' customers**

- **People who have purchased products or services that complement your products or services**

- **People who hang around others who purchase products and services that you sell**

They don't have any money.

The No Money argument can be very confusing. Very often, a prospect will use the excuse that they don't have the money. Telling a salesperson you cannot afford something is an easy way to get rid of the pesky salesperson. As a society, we have been trained to do this, because no one likes a pesky salesperson.

But by the same token you need to fish in the pond that has the most fish. If you sell a high-end product, such as a Mercedes, you need to target people who have incomes high enough to afford a Mercedes. If you're selling carpet cleaning, don't send mailers to low income neighborhoods who probably can't afford to have their carpets cleaned. Be smart about your target market. **You will hear me say this over and over, but choosing the right target market is the single most important key to success in marketing, closely followed by repetition.**

Assuming you are fishing in the right pond, it is extremely important to create a value proposition that will get people to get by the price objection, and see that the value provided is worth the money they pay.

They don't need the product right now.

This is an area that you can easily overcome with an effective marketing campaign. Your job is to create a sense of urgency, using deadlines and scarcity, along with repetitive touches, to urge the person to act now versus wait. It is a natural tendency for most people to procrastinate. By sending a series of regular mailings, showing how the deadline is fast approaching and is about to expire, you can often get someone off their butt to act, when they would've normally done nothing.

Multistep marketing campaigns are extremely effective in overcoming procrastination.

They don't trust you.

The fear of loss is one of the strongest motivating factors to do nothing. Fear of loss means people are afraid they're going to be taken. There so many rip-off artists in the world that we are naturally skeptical of anyone that offers something that sounds too good to be true. Your job as a marketer is to alleviate those fears by taking away the risk. There are several methods you can use to take away the risk:

- **Guarantees of performance**
- **Money-back guarantees**
- **Free trials**
- **Free gifts that they can keep even if they choose to return the product**
- **Testimonials from satisfied customers**
- **Easy communication with your staff**
- **Give something to them before taking their money, and also after. Not just free gifts, but access to you, free advice, extra bonuses that they didn't expect.**

They are already buying your product or service from someone else and they are happy.

This one seems hard to overcome, but is actually not. In today's world, it is very rare for a company to consistently provide excellent products and services year after year. Even the best suppliers often make mistakes. Or, customers change, and the service provider doesn't change with them. Companies often take their customers for granted, and after a while customers often feel ignored and may be enticed by a new company.

If you've chosen your target market wisely, a person who is happy with someone else might be on your list. Regular marketing to them over a period of time will build your name in their subconscious, and just might give you a shot one day in the future. Your goal as a marketer is to stay in front of someone often enough that they think of you the next time they're ready to purchase your product or service.

Regular Direct Mail Marketing is a very effective tool for this purpose.

Again, let me use an example in the real estate investing field. As a real estate investor, your goal is to buy properties at a low enough price that you can make a profit after covering all your purchase, repair, and sales costs. Most people do not want to sell their house for a price that is far below the market value. Your challenge as a marketer is to overcome most people's assumption that the need to hire a real estate agent and sell in the traditional manner.

For you to have a chance to get a sale, you need to show the value in what you provide so that accepting an offer far below the market value, without the help of a real estate agent, feels good to the client. You do this by talking about avoiding repair costs, inspections, hassles, real estate fees, holding costs, and pain-and-suffering. You monetize all these issues to show that your offer really is not low when you consider all the factors. These types of things can be done with effective marketing copy.

Another effective method, is to be the backup supplier. If a person is using your product or service, but using another supplier, and they're happy, you don't want to try to tell them that they're not happy. That would only make you look bad and question their decision-making.

Instead, congratulate the current supplier for doing a good job, and then assure the prospect that if that supplier ever stops doing a good job, you'll be ready to step in and take over. This is a longer-term strategy, but can be done effectively with Direct Mail.

Chapter 3

Key Elements
to Success in Marketing

I'm assuming you now understand the importance of being an expert marketer. Before you can decide if Online or Direct Mail Marketing makes sense for you, you need to understand the basic elements of any marketing campaign.

There are ten key elements to every successful Direct Marketing campaign. These elements are true both for Offline and Online Marketing. Unfortunately, most people miss out on some, if not all, of these key characteristics.

Key Element #1
Have a Unique Selling Proposition (USP)

Dan Kennedy is one of the greatest marketing geniuses of the last 30 years, and I will quote him when it comes to defining a USP. Dan says, "What is it that you do that would make the customer choose you over anyone else, including doing nothing? And you can't use price, quality, or service."

You have to ZIG when everyone else ZAGS. What is your ZIG?

Everybody claims to offer the lowest prices, the best quality, and the best service. Consumers have come to expect that from everyone. It is not unique. What is it that you do that sets you apart from your competition?

Dan uses the example of Domino's pizza. Dominoes never talk about how good their pizza was, the quality of their ingredients, or anything else about the pizza. All they said was, "Hot pizza delivered in 30 minutes or less, guaranteed." Good pizza was not part of the equation. They built an empire on the promise to deliver it within 30 minutes. The customers cared more about the speed than they did about anything else.

Finding your unique selling proposition is perhaps the most difficult thing for any business to do. As a real estate investor, you buy houses for cash, just like everyone else. Almost all of your competitors offer the same thing. Does this sound familiar?

> We will buy your house for cash.
>
> No real estate commissions.
>
> No repairs.
>
> We will close fast.

Everyone is saying the same thing. What can you do that makes you stand out from the hundreds of other people all saying the same thing?

A more compelling USP is **"We Buy Ugly Houses."** It uniquely differentiates the offer from all the others in the industry.

Maybe you come up with a unique guarantee. Maybe you give your service a name that stands out. Maybe you have a slightly different approach than your competitors. Think about what you do and how you do it and find a way to differentiate yourself.

One example in the real estate space is the headline, "I will sell your house in 90 days or less or I'll buy it myself." That truly is a unique, compelling message for anyone interested in selling their house.

Once you've decided how you are unique, you need to build your marketing message around that USP.

Checklist for Identifying USP

Below is a list of topics that will help you to identify what is unique about your product or service. Remember saying that you have the best price, quality, or service does not count.

- **Unique Name**
- **competitive positioning**
- **exclusive niche**
- **affinity**
- **hidden benefit**
- **method of marketing and distribution**
- **continuity**
- **membership**
- **service difference**
- **added value**

- **premiums/gift with purchase**
- **packaging difference**
- **size**
- **expertise**
- **price**
- **payment terms**
- **guarantee**
- **celebrity**
- **combination**

Key Element #2
Identify Your Target Market Or Client

Perhaps the greatest thing about Direct Mail Marketing is that it is very easy to target specific demographic groups. You can rent lists that contain just about any criteria you can imagine about a market. On the consumer side, it is common to look for specific ZIP Codes, income levels, the value of homes, equity in your home, type of family, size of family, owners or renters, and a myriad of other demographic factors.

On the commercial side, you would look for SIC codes, size of business, number of employees, location, annual sales, etc.

Who should you target?

Choosing the right list is vital to the success of a direct marketing campaign. You can mail the greatest offer in the world to the wrong list and get zero response. You can also mail a mediocre offer to a good list and still get a good response.

There are three main types of targets that every business should approach:

1) **Your in-house customer list**

2) **Your in-house prospect list**

3) **Your targeted cold prospect list**

The in-house customer list is obvious. It is simply a list of your customers. So many marketers take this list for granted and don't do anything with their customers. Never forget your in-house customer list, as it is just as important as any other list you may use.

The in-house prospect list contains prospects who have contacted you in the past about your product or service, but have not bought from you. The fact that they already took a step to contact you puts you closer to a sale. Just because they haven't bought yet doesn't mean they don't like you. They may still be thinking about it. Maybe you didn't do a good enough job of showing them the value proposition, and can do a better job the second time around. Maybe they never really saw your materials even though they inquired. Maybe you just did a lousy job the first time around. No matter what the reason, this is a very valuable list.

The third list is a targeted cold prospect list.

This one is a little more difficult to obtain, and you have to put on your thinking cap to figure out who exactly should be on this list. In order to do this, you have to identify who is your ideal target customer, and what are some the demographics associated with them. Then go to sources where you can find people who meet those criteria. There are mailing list companies, magazines, associations, clubs, trade groups, and all sorts of sources for people with similar demographics.

A good example of this in the real estate business would be choosing high equity properties. Let's say you do not target your list properly, and most of the people you mail to have very little equity in their property. To make money as a real estate investor, you have to purchase houses at wholesale value, often 50 cents on the dollar or less. If you offer a person who owes $100,000 on their house $50,000, there is almost no chance they're going to say yes. You may even get a 10% response rate to the mailer, because you have a compelling offer. But if none of those people are the right prospects, you will not get any deals. You are wasting your money even soliciting those types of people.

But it's not enough just to target cold prospects.

Key Element #3
Have An Irresistible Offer

An irresistible offer is the lifeblood of any marketing campaign. So many people make a mistake of sending out a mail piece, email, or website that has no offer at all. Typically people will say, "We are in the _____ business and here's our phone number." That is not an offer.

It is critical to determine what your objective is, and then craft an offer to help you achieve that objective. If your goal is to generate a lead, an example of an irresistible offer might be, "Call today for your free report on how to maximize profits in your business." An even stronger offer might be, "Call me today for a no obligation cash offer on your house."

So many people make the mistake of only listing features and benefits, but they are missing a compelling offer. *Remember, to say "We clean carpets" and list a phone number is NOT an offer.*

Key Element #4
Always Talk In Terms Of Benefits To The Prospect To Solve Their Key Problem

Any time you write anything on any sort of marketing piece, ask the question, "Who cares?" When I say who cares, I mean look at it from the prospect's point of view. If the prospect doesn't care about what you just said, don't say it.

Let's look at the real estate business again. What is a typical problem someone might have? They may have a vacant house that is costing them money, and they don't know what to do. Think about that problem when you craft your message. You might say, "We will remove all the worry and hassle of fixing up and getting your vacant house ready for sale, so you can move on and enjoy your family." A statement like that is solving their key problem by talking about the benefit to them.

Another example is what I used to get people interested in this book. I know that most small business owners are interested in more sales and profits. All my marketing copy talked about the benefits of increased profits - not about Direct Mail specifically. They don't care about doing Direct Mail without knowing what Direct Mail is going to do for them. Connecting the fact that effective Direct Mail can result in increased profits makes sense to most business owners.

Key Element #5
Create A Sense Of Urgency

Sense of urgency is very important in any marketing piece but especially a Direct Mail piece. Create a sense of urgency by creating a specific time or a specific deadline. You can create scarcity with, "This offer is limited to the first 10 people! Respond within 48 hours!" or "We are only buying one house in your neighborhood." Sense of urgency motivates the reader to act. It is human nature to not want to miss out. The more you can make it feel like the reader will be missing out, the stronger your message will be.

Key Element #6
Include A Call To Action

A call to action tells them exactly what to do and when to do it. "Pick up the phone and call our office today" is a very simple call to action. You might say, "Go to our website and fill out the form today." Working in the call to action with the sense of urgency is a powerful duo.

Key Element #7
Include A Guarantee

If you can't guarantee what you sell,
you'd better find a different business.

Having a guarantee takes the risk away from the prospect. Most people do not like take any risk, especially when it comes to receiving a solicitation in the mail. This is also true of online solicitations. We all have an inherent distrust of people trying to get our money, so guarantees go a long way to help relieve that distrust. The stronger your guarantee can be, the stronger response rates will be. The strongest guarantee is always a 100% money back guarantee. However, that is not always possible in every sale situation. For instance, if someone was unhappy with a real estate transaction, there is no way there is no way you could guarantee their money back.

What you *can* do is guarantee various elements of the transaction. For instance, here are some ideas.

I guarantee I will call you back in 24 hours.

I guarantee I'll fix anything that goes wrong for the first year.

I guarantee I'll show up with money on your doorstep at the time I make the offer.

I guarantee I'll call you back with a smile on my face.

I guarantee you will have no hassles and the transaction will close quickly.

There are all kinds of things you can do with guarantees to strengthen your offer.

Key Element #8
Have A Follow-Up System In Place

All the previous elements dealt with the mail piece itself. However, it is just as critical to have an effective follow-up system in place. Getting a bunch of responses to a mail piece is a complete waste of money if you don't follow up properly. This means when you first get a response, you need to have a way to do something that really gets the attention of the prospect. You might send them a "shock-and-awe" kit. A "shock-and-awe" kit is a box of goodies the prospect would never expect to get from anyone in the situation. You might make a personal appearance. A phone call from the president. Anything you can do to tell the prospect you care is a good thing.

Beyond the initial contact, you also need to have an ongoing follow-up system in place. An email auto-responder would be effective in this case. But you can also do it with additional Direct Mail pieces. Maybe a quarterly newsletter. Maybe periodic phone calls. Whatever works for your market to ensure that people remember you is good.

Key Element #9
Repetition Is Everything

Another key element is repetition. Repetition is King. If you think you can do one mail piece or one email campaign and set profit records, you're dreaming. In the case of real estate it's a fact that about 7% of the population moves every year. There's probably another 7% thinking about moving in any given time. That's only about 14% of the people who probably have any interest at all in hearing about selling their house. 14% means 14 out of 100, which means 86 out of 100 are not interested at all right now.

Next year another 7% of people are going to move and probably another 7% will be thinking about moving, so just because they're not interested this year does not mean they won't be interested next year. Your goal as a marketer is to put your name in front of people often enough so that when it finally comes time for them to act on your offer, they think of you first before they think of your competition.

Here's a rule of thumb. Whatever response you get from one mailer, you can at least double the response by doing two additional mail pieces. In other words, if you send the same thing three times to the same list, you'll typically get double the response you would get over just one mailing.

Another rule of thumb in Direct Mail is if an offer works, mail it again and again until it stops working. It is not uncommon to mail the same offer up to 10 times before it finally gets to the point where it's no longer profitable to mail.

This is especially true in the real estate investing market these days. There are hundreds, if not thousands, of gurus traveling the country putting on weekend seminars teaching people how to flip houses. Every one of these guys teaches people to mail small postcards and simple handwritten letters to find houses to buy. They're also teaching people to look for high equity homes in certain areas, and all the students are being taught the same thing. They're even being pushed to the same web services who offer the same postcards to all different types of people.

Most of these people will not succeed. They will do one mail piece, and never repeat. By hitting the prospect several times, ideally with mail pieces a little different than your competition, you'll begin to build a brand with the recipient and they may begin to remember you. If you use the eight previous elements, you will stand out from most of your competition, because very few of them are doing these things.

So Remember: Mail, Mail, Mail, And Then Mail Some More!

Key Element #10
Track Your Results

Failure to track results is perhaps the biggest mistake most marketers make. They will spend thousands of dollars on campaigns, but fail to put the systems in place to know who responded to those campaigns. Without proper tracking mechanisms, there is no way to know what worked and what didn't work. Successful marketers are constantly testing and tweaking their campaigns to continually improve.

There are various ways to track campaigns. If your offer is a phone call, the simplest way is to have the person answering the phone ask them where they heard about your product or service. The problem with this method is people often forget to do that or they don't write it down, and before you know it you don't have the proper information.

Another way to do that is to get a tracking phone number. There are systems that allow you to buy phone numbers and use a specific phone number for a specific mail piece so you know the call that came in on that line could've only been from that mail piece. This is a good system but doing this for every mail piece individually can be challenging. It is a little easier to break up your mailings into groups or campaigns, then assign an individual phone number to a campaign.

Another method is to send people to a website that is a specific landing page for your specific offer. This is an excellent way to track, but does involve creating different landing pages for each mail piece. Again, if you don't have an easy system to do this, it can be challenging. What often happens is people get in a hurry and they skip this step.

Perhaps the easiest method is to have a specific response device in the mail piece that gets mailed or faxed back to you. Some people consider this to be old-fashioned marketing, but it is very effective for tracking and some people still prefer to do business this way.

The optimal solution is to have a system that involves several of these elements, and takes very little time to set up for each mailing. At Graphic Connections Group, we have such a system.

You can reach us by calling 636-519-8320 or going to our website www.gcgmail.com.

Chapter 4

More on Targeting the Perfect Client

Targeting your ideal customer is perhaps the most important thing in marketing. As I said earlier, you can still get a decent response sending a poor marketing message to a good list. But it is almost impossible to get a good response, no matter how good your marketing message is, to the wrong list. So let's talk about how to identify the best list.

When I talk about lists, it is obvious that you need a specific list to send out Direct Mail pieces or emails. But targeting is also important for all types of marketing including print advertising, radio advertising and TV advertising. It is much harder to use mass media to target, because it hits a wider audience. However, there are some things you can do to at least partially target your audience.

First you have to identify the ideal customer. Take a look at your existing customers. In just about every business you have good customers and bad customers. The good customers are the people who are always friendly, easy to do business with, pay your prices without complaint, and keep coming back over and over. Many times you consider these customers your friends.

The bad customers are difficult to work with, complain a lot, are always questioning prices and beating you down, and generally a pain in the butt. Typically you dread taking the phone calls from these customers. Often, it actually costs you money to do business with them.

In crafting your marketing message, smart people will target only people who fit the profile of the ideal customer. So how do you figure out what that profile is?

Every business is different; you have to use a little common sense here. Look at things like age or gender. Are they married or single? Are they business owners or do they work for someone else? Are they conservative or liberal politically? Are they price shoppers, or do they value quality and are willing to pay for it? What type of products do they buy? Are they large orders or small orders? Are they a pleasure to talk to, or a pain? Where do they live? Is geography an issue? Is it important that they are close to your office?

It costs the same to market to lousy prospects as it does to good prospects. So why not spend your money targeting only people who have the best chance of becoming good customers?

The second part of this project is to identify who you want your ideal customer to be. Looking at your existing customers is a good starting point, but if your business is not making money, or if you're not having fun, maybe it's because you're targeting the wrong people to start with. Just because you have existing customers doesn't mean it is profitable or they are the right customers.

Maybe you need to completely revamp who your target market is. Write down the characteristics of your ideal client. Compare that to your best existing customers and see if they are similar. If they are, you have your answer. If they are not, you need to do some serious soul-searching to decide where it is you want to go in the future.

Life is too short to not enjoy your time at work. Why put yourself in a position to be unhappy, being forced to deal with people who stress you out? Why not spend your time searching for people who will make it a joy to work every day?

Once you have identified your ideal target prospect, it is time to find out where you can find them. The first and most obvious place is to call a mailing list provider and ask them if they have lists of people who fit the demographic profile you are looking for. If they don't have an exact match, ask them if they can find something close. Mailing list brokers can easily find characteristics such as location, gender, marital status, household income and home values. This information is easily available for most mailing lists. Generally speaking the more selectors you add, the more the list costs.

If you want to drill down even further, some lists have information about buying habits, magazine subscriptions, credit card users, credit profiles, and other demographic information. But this type of information is not quite as easy to obtain from every list. It all depends on where the list came from and the type of information provided.

You can also look towards associations, clubs, and magazines for lists. For instance, if you are in the auto parts business, there's a good chance your customers might subscribe to auto magazines. You can also look at other competitors who are selling to your market, might have noncompeting products, and might be willing to rent you their list.

Be creative and think, *Where can I find people whose profiles look like my ideal customer?*

Chapter 5

Mailing List Basics

Your mailing list is an extremely important part of your marketing program, especially when you're using Direct Mail Marketing. Once you've identified your ideal customer, now it is time to evaluate the different sources to get the data. As I mentioned earlier, the first and most obvious place is to go to a mailing list provider. This is a company, such as infoUSA, USAdata, or MelisaaData, whose entire business is to provide mailing lists.

Ask a few basic questions to make sure that the data you're getting is as good as possible:

How often is the data updated?

Reputable companies update their data at least monthly. Ideally, you want a list with extremely fresh data, but that is not always possible based on the source of the data. Many real lists that look at property data originate from property tax records. Different municipalities operate on different schedules, and their data can be 6 to 12 months old. However, that may be your only choice.

Does the list guarantee deliverability?

(Deliverability is the ability of the mail piece to be successfully delivered to the prospect.) The answer should be yes, but again, depending on how fresh the data is, this may be impossible to guarantee. A 90% deliverability rating is generally acceptable in the Direct Mail business. That means up to 10% of the addresses might come back as undeliverable.

10% seems high.

Yes it does, but let me explain why it is so high. All reputable list providers use software programs to CASS certify, and also run the list through the National Change of Address (NCOA) database to try to ensure the best possible deliverability. Reputable mail houses do the same thing just prior to dropping a mailing. CASS certification looks at the address formatting and ensures that the street, city, state and zip code are properly formatted, and that the address does exist in the postal database. The program will modify the address if possible to make sure it is valid. This program does not check the name against the address, only the address. In other words, we know this is a legitimate house, we just don't know who lives in the house.

NCOA is the database managed by the post office that shows everyone who has moved in the last several years. The post office will forward mail for up to a year if you fill out their postcard and tell them you are moving. After a year, they will no longer forward the mail but the data is included in the NCOA database.

The problem is not everyone who moves informs the post office. They should, but they don't. You might think it's pretty stupid not to inform the post office you are moving. However, there are a lot of people who are happy to run away from their mail. Maybe bill collectors are chasing them. Or maybe they're just not very organized. If they don't tell the post office they're moving, the post office has no way of adding that data to the NCOA database.

Roughly 7% of the population moves every year. Even if a list company updates its data every month, they have no way of updating it if the people who move don't do their part to inform the system that they have moved.

A secondary issue is that people sometimes use false names to order things, or middle names instead of first names, or purposely misspell names. Data is only as good as its accuracy.

Another problem can happen at the point of data entry. If the person entering the data is not careful, names can be butchered. This can cause the mail to be delivered to the wrong place. The homeowner can also reject the mail and return it to the post office, saying it is not his or hers.

The last thing that happens is that the mailman delivers it to the wrong place. This is more common than you think. When a letter goes to the wrong house, some people throw it in the trash, and some people return it to the mail driver saying it's not their mail. Rather than trying to deliver it to the proper address, the postman usually just returns it as undeliverable.

Add up all these factors, and you can see why getting a 10% undeliverable rate is not that surprising.

Don't get hung up on undeliverable mail. I know it is frustrating when you do a mailing and you get a big pile of undeliverables coming back to you. You feel like you're wasting your money. What really matters is return on investment, not how many undeliverables you get. If your mailing is profitable, don't worry about the undeliverables.

That doesn't mean you have to be stupid with your money either. If you plan to use the list more than once, take the time to go through the list and delete all of the undeliverables prior to doing a second mailing. This way you won't repeat the problem. Managing and cleaning up your list is also a smart thing to do in your overall marketing program.

Can I use a list over and over again?

Different list companies have different policies. Most companies that are in the list business will have two different rates. They will have a one-time use rate and an unlimited use rate. Typically the unlimited use cost is about 50% higher than the one-time use cost. Most major list compilers do charge for unlimited use. If a list broker tells you something different, be a little suspicious and dig more to find out where he or she is getting the list.

There are private list sources that may only charge you one fee no matter if it's a single use or multiple uses. It is very important that you clarify this prior to buying a list. You can get into trouble if you violate the policy.

Don't get hung up on the cost of the list. Just like identifying your ideal prospect is critical to your success, getting a list of those prospects is equally critical. Paying a few pennies more for a good list will pay for itself many times over. Too many people made the mistake of going for the low bid list, only to be disappointed to find out it was garbage. Remember, the list will be the least expensive part of your marketing campaign, even if you pay premium price for it. Don't be a cheapskate when it comes to buying lists.

Chapter 6

Using Offline to
Promote Online and Vice-Versa

One of the most powerful marketing strategies you can use is to combine offline Direct Mail Marketing with Online Marketing. In Online Marketing, you place ads or send emails directing people to a landing page, opt-in page, or squeeze page on a website. (Landing pages, opt in pages, and squeeze pages are all terms for a webpage that forces the visitor to fill something out to get further information or move to the next step.) Once the person fills out the information on the landing or squeeze page, they are entered into an email auto-responder series and sales funnel.

The same thing can be done with Direct Mail. Initially send out a mail piece that drives a person to an online landing page or squeeze page, and the online sales funnel takes over from there. If you already have an online system that has numbers that will work financially, it is extremely easy to also make that work offline. The beauty of this is it expands your prospect base. It also brings in a whole new element of potential customers who may not be people you could find online.

There are several different ways you can choose to market combining Direct Mail with Online Marketing. One option is to use your Direct Mail campaign to drive people to an opt-in page where your sole objective is to get the prospect to give you their name and email. The prospect will then be entered into an auto-responder series through which you present your product or service. At the same time, the prospect will be redirected to a webpage, the next step in your sales funnel. It is extremely important to offer the prospect something of value in exchange for opting in. It can be a free special report, book, newsletter, or other offer that is compelling.

Postcards or short letters are used for this type of marketing. The postcard's job is to drive someone to the webpage, and let the webpage do the selling. Typically the postcard will have a headline, an irresistible offer which will get them to the webpage, and then a call to action with instructions. Often there is an option to either make a phone call, or go to a webpage.

Another method is to do more selling on the sales letter, webpage, or both. This is more of a one-step sales process. You still use a webpage in the process, but hopefully the prospect is already sold on your product when they go to the webpage. If they're not, the webpage also has sales copy, and an order form. Instead of just asking for information for further follow-up, you're actually selling your product or service on that webpage. A good strategy is to introduce a small sale, typically less than $50. After the person has made the initial purchase, you will upsell them into more expensive programs.

In all of these cases, the email auto-responder is a vital element to success. An auto-responder is a tool that lets you preprogram a series of email messages that will go out on your chosen schedule to each prospect. The beauty of an auto-responder is that once you write all the messages, the entire thing happens automatically. It is an automated way to stay in front of clients. And since the client was at least semi-interested in your product or service, hopefully they will pay a little closer attention to the emails, instead of deleting them before looking at them.

Chapter 7

Add an Online Kicker
to Increase Response Rates
Even More

We have been speaking about using offline tools to drive Online Marketing. We can kick this up a notch with this simple trick. Technically we are focusing on the online portion of the strategy, but it is especially attractive when using Direct Mail to drive traffic.

One of the latest and most effective online techniques, used by more and more marketers, is the use of re-marketing or re-targeting ads. These are ads that will follow an online user from one website to another.

Let me explain. Let's say you send out a Direct Mail piece, and direct a person to a landing page. At that point, the person has the choice of filling out the opt-in box on that page, or just going to another website. Most people will move on without filling out the opt-in box. In the past, there was no way to capture that lead. If they went away without opting in, they were lost forever.

Not anymore.

Using retargeting technology, the system will apply cookies or pixels to the computer of the visitor. Those cookies will follow them to whatever website they visit. Attached to those cookies are ads for your particular product or service. When the person goes to other websites that allow these types of ads, the ads will pop up on their screen. They call that 'impressions.' One extremely effective way to boost your response rates of any marketing campaign, online or offline, is to utilize this re-marketing technology. These ads will follow the user around for as long as you are willing to pay.

The benefit is twofold. First, the cost of these ads is relatively inexpensive, and there are systems out there that automate this process and make it very simple. Second, this gives you a much greater chance of getting the prospect's attention, as they will be hit multiple times with your offer. It's no longer over if they leave your website without opting in.

This is one of the most powerful technologies available online today. Combining that with a Direct Mail campaign can dramatically increase the response rates of your campaign.

Graphic Connections Group has one of those systems, and it has proven to be a very powerful tool to increase results from Direct Mail campaigns. Give us a call to find out more details about a specific system that is already set up to drive more leads to you than ever before.

Chapter 8

Profit Results Matter,
NOT Response Rates

One of the biggest mistakes marketers make, especially in the direct-mail world, is getting hung up on percent response rates versus return on investment. I can't tell you how many times I've been asked, "What kind of response rate can I expect to get on this mailing?" Although it is a practical question, it is only one part of the question they should be asking. The second part is, "What is your typical closing rate on a lead, and how much money do you make on a typical deal?"

There is no average response rate. That number does not exist. Response rates can be anywhere from zero to as high as 100%. Yes, it is true that most mailings do fall into the lower end of that spectrum, and it is not unusual to get less than a 2% response on a mailing. But there's still no average.

There are so many factors that affect response rate that is not possible to boil it all down to an overall average across all industries and campaigns. The quality of the list, the quality of the mail piece, timeliness, whether or not the mail piece has the proper offer, call to action, and guarantee are all factors that play into the response rate. The quality of the mail piece has a huge impact as well. The smaller your mailing, the harder it is to get averages that make statistical sense. If you only mail 250 pieces of mail every month for year, it would not be surprising to get zero response on one mailing and 25 responses on the next. You need at least 5,000 mailers to be able to get an average that means anything.

The best thing you can do is to track a cumulative response rate when you're dealing with a lot of small mailings. When you get a statistically valid number, then you can start to test other mail pieces against that to see if you can improve on the numbers.

Another huge factor that affects response rates is your objective. Asking for someone to call you for more information, or to respond for free report, is a lot easier than trying to make an actual sale with your mail-piece. In addition, the higher the price, the lower the response rates tend to be.

Here's a rule of thumb. If you're trying to make a sale with your mail piece, and you're going to cold prospects, keep the offer under $100 for best results. Once they have made that initial purchase, then you can upsell them on more expensive offers. If you're selling to existing clients, your offer can range between $79, and $800. Anything over $800 normally requires some sort of personal contact in addition to the mail piece. If you try to sell items higher than $800 you're going to find it extremely difficult to sell in a one-step mailing.

Let's Get Back To Results

I'm not saying not to worry about your response rates, but the other two factors (closing rate and profit per sale)are equally if not more important. It is those three factors, combined together, along with considering the cost of the marketing program, that allow you to calculate the return on investment.

Let's say you mail 1,000 pieces of mail, and receive a 2% response rate, which consisted of people interested in your service. Let's also assume your typical sale nets you $10,000 profit. I'm also going to assume that for every 10 leads you get, you typically close one of those deals.

If you get a 2% response rate on 1,000 pieces of mail, that is 20 leads. If you can close 10% of those leads, that is two deals. If you make $10,000 per deal, that is $20,000 profit you made on this campaign. If you spent $1,000 on the campaign and you earned $20,000 profit, that is a 20 to 1 return on investment. I think just about anyone would repeat that campaign with those kinds of numbers.

Now let's take that same example and assume you only got a 1% response rate, but you still got a 10% closing rate and still made $10,000 per deal. That would be 10 leads with one deal, earning you $10,000. The mail piece still cost you $10,00 so you still made a 10 to 1 return on investment. Still an excellent return.

Now let's look at this another way. Instead of focusing so much on response rates, let's focus on increasing your closing ratio. If you could take your closing ratio from 10%, to 20%, you can double your profits with the same number of leads. How much would you be willing to spend on the 20 leads you have, to increase your closing ratio from 2 to 4 on the 20? It's a lot easier to improve closing rates than it is to increase response rates.

Lifetime Value Of The Customer Is A HUGE Factor To Consider

Spending more money than you take in on the initial campaign is not necessarily a bad thing. If the lifetime value of your customer provides an adequate rate of return, it still may make sense to do a marketing campaign, even though the initial numbers may not be all that exciting.

Let's say that on the initial sale, you only make $1,000 for your product or service. However, a good customer will spend $1,000 per year with you. Let's also say that a typical customer stays with you for five years. The lifetime value of a customer in this scenario is 5 × $1,000, or $5,000.

If your initial mailing campaign cost $1,000 and you only make $1,000 on the first order, that is still a good deal. In years two through five, you're going to get $4,000 more with no marketing cost.

In most businesses, if you can break even on the initial marketing, and you do have a product where there is a repeat business factor, then the lifetime value of the customer turns what might seem like losing marketing campaigns into winners.

Chapter 9

Types of Direct Mail

Format is very important in Direct Mail. When talking about format, I mean what the mail piece looks like. Different formats have different purposes.

The Rule of 3-30

The second most common thing everybody does at the end of the day is go to the pile of mail. The first is going to the bathroom. When you arrive home every day to get your big pile of mail that's waiting in your mailbox, most people sort through it quickly and decide what they're going to keep and what they're going to throw in the trash.

Typically, people will take three seconds to decide if they're going to keep the mail or throw it away. And then they take 30 seconds for them to decide if they're going to look more carefully at your particular mail piece. Thus you have the rule of 3-30.

The format of your Direct Mail piece can dramatically impact whether you pass the 3-30 test.

For the purposes of our discussion, we will focus on five main types of Direct Mail: postcards, letters, self-mailers, priority or special delivery mail, and lumpy mail.

Each of these types of mail has its place, depending on the strategy you're trying to invoke.

POSTCARDS

The post office's definition of a postcard is a single sheet of thick cardstock paper, ranging in size from 3.5 x 5 inches to 4.25 x 6 inches. It can be printed in full color on both sides, black and white on both sides, or a combination of the two. The design can be simple type in black and white, full-color with pictures, or anything in between.

Many printers say it is also common to see postcards much larger than that. You'll see them as large as 6 x 11 inches in your mailbox. In fact, with the advent of every door Direct Mail, you'll even see sizes much larger than that. However, when you have a postcard larger than 4.25 x 6 inches, you get kicked up into the letter category for postage. For the purposes of our discussion, we will use the term postcard for all single sheet mailers no matter what the size. Just keep in mind as your postcards get larger, the postage gets more expensive.

In general, when people use the small 4.25 x 6 inch postcards, there is not enough room to make a sale. People who use those are typically looking for someone to respond for more information about the product or service. It is still important to have a compelling offer, but your offer is focused on the next step. Don't try to make the sale. Just get the prospect to take the next step.

It is up to the person sending the postcard to handle responses in a way that leads to sales. In general, the larger the postcard, the better the response. Why is this? If you go back to the beginning of this book, you'll note that I talked about how many people will sort their mail over the trashcan. As they are sorting the mail over the trashcan, the items that are bigger naturally stand out. An oversized postcard that is 6 x 11 inches definitely stands out in the mail. It allows you a better chance to get someone's attention before they throw it away.

It is possible to have a longer sales message on the larger postcards, and to make an actual sale from them, but it is difficult. It is still best used as a device to encourage someone to respond for more information.

As a general rule, larger postcards pull, or perform, better than smaller postcards. The only exception to that is two mail drops of small postcards will out-pull one large postcard. However, if you go to two mail drops of large postcards, it will out-pull two mail drops of small postcards.

The benefit to using postcards is that the recipient can see the marketing message without having to open an envelope. There are many marketers who believe this makes them extremely effective. Fancy designs are not always necessary to get a good postcard response. In the real estate business, we have found that the simple, clearly worded postcards seem to pull better than postcards with fancy graphics. We have had especially good success with postcards that look like an important notice.

Another strategy is to use a postcard that looks like a handwritten note.

The only way to really find out what works for you is to test.

SELF-MAILERS

Self-mailers consist of a piece of paper that is folded, and usually tabbed, and is mailed without an envelope. It can be on a text weigh paper or card stock.

The advantage of self-mailers is that you avoid the cost of an envelope, and the cost of stuffing the mail into an envelope. Typically, this means the mail is a little cheaper. You can do some fairly creative things with self-mailers, and they usually will get opened if done correctly. A disadvantage is that it is easy for self-mailers to get chewed up in the mail.

With the self-mailer, you can add teaser copy on the outside, or make it look very personal like a handwritten note or invitation. Your imagination is the limit.

LETTERS

Letters consist of a piece of paper with either a handwritten or typed message, folded into an envelope. You can use varying sizes of envelopes.

There are two schools of thought in letter mailing. The first is trying to make the envelope look like a personal letter from a friend or family. Using things like handwritten fonts, live stamps, applied return address labels, blue or red ink, invitation style envelopes, or colored envelopes all help to make things look more personal. The job of the envelope is to get the person to open it. That's it. Once the person opens the envelope, it has done its job and the focus is on what is inside.

The second school of thought is to make the envelope look like it contains something extremely important. You could even make it look like it came from a bank or the IRS. There are all kinds of strategies used to make things look important..

A third strategy is to use teaser copy on the outside of the envelope. Teaser copy is printing on the outside of the envelope, whose goal it is to get the person to open the envelope and look inside. This method is a bit more challenging, because if your teaser copy is not particularly compelling, the envelope will likely go straight to the trash. Most people do not like to read obvious junk mail. Envelopes with teaser copy are usually obvious junk mail.

In general, I prefer to use the personalized approach in most cases. Our clients use two main types of letter mailers. One is a handwritten yellow letter, with a handwritten font on the outside envelope. The other is a typed business letter with a business font on the envelope and a look of importance.

PRIORITY/SPECIAL DELIVERY MAIL

Here we are talking about envelopes that stand out above and beyond normal plain envelopes. Examples are FedEx overnight envelopes, UPS Next Day Air, or simulated envelopes that are made to look like they contain important documents. Usually these envelopes are made of cardboard and/or at least 9 x 12 inches in size.

There is no question these types of envelopes get opened. It is a rare person who is going to throw away an envelope like this without a least checking out what's inside first. The drawback is that the postage is quite a bit more for these types of envelopes. If you're using actual FedEx or UPS overnight envelopes, or even FedEx Ground, it is not unusual to spend between $7 and $30 per envelope for the mail piece. You had better have an exciting offer with a high end profit, to justify spending that much money on an envelope.

Many companies, including mine, have designed envelopes to simulate these overnight envelopes, but are far cheaper to mail. In addition, we have developed standard mail postage methods, which allow us to spend far less money on postage on these larger envelopes. However, even with all those strategies in place, they are still far more expensive to mail than postcards or letters.

Remember, the job of the envelope is to get the customer to open the mail. Once it is open, it is the contents inside that take center stage. So if you're going to spend the money on one of these more expensive envelopes, you'd better have an offer that is irresistible and will lead you to some very profitable sales.

LUMPY MAIL

Lumpy mail is mail that literally has a lump in it. There are all kinds of unusual items that you can mail. It might be a trash can with a letter crumpled up inside. It might be a bank bag that has a letter inside. It might be a large poster rolled up in a tube, a Frisbee with a message on it, a boomerang, or any other creative thing you can think of.

I mentioned earlier that it's possible to get a 100% response rate. A man named John Goldman mailed a watermelon through the mail to a hand-selected mailing list. He literally put stamps on an actual watermelon, and taped a mailing label to it, and mailed it through the US mail. They accepted it and delivered it, and 100% of the recipients who received that watermelon took the action that John requested.

It worked because it was so outrageous that the people getting it could not help but respond.

The benefit of lumpy mail is that it gets opened 100% of the time. There is no way a person is going to receive a piece of lumpy mail and ignore it. It gets noticed because it naturally has to be on the top of the mail pile just because it's lumpy.

There's no question that lumpy mail costs more to send. But again, as I mentioned before in this book, you cannot just focus on one aspect of the project. You have to focus on the return on investment.

I have another example of a lumpy mail piece to illustrate this point. I recently received a box in the mail that was about a half inch thick, and the size of a small book. It came in a Fedex letter mailer. It looked like a book with a thick cover. When I opened the page, it contained a small video screen and the video automatically started playing with a message that contained an offer. It was so cool I watched the entire six minute video. This particular offer was an invitation to attend a very high-end networking or "mastermind" group, and the price was $1,000. The initial video asked me to call them, which I did. I spoke to a salesman, who easily talked me into the $1,000 price point. He also told me that if I was happy with the mastermind group, the ultimate price would be $10,000.

I accepted his offer, attended the meeting, liked it, and ended up spending the $10,000. This particular group was focused on marketing, and the leader used this example as part of our discussion on effective marketing campaigns. He told us he sent it to 100 people, and he spent $25 for each video plus another $20 per person to mail it overnight. That is $45 per person, or $4,500 total for 100 people, just to mail the offer. 25 of those people chose the introductory offer for $1,000. So his initial investment, which seemed really high at $45 per mail piece, seemed like chump change when you consider he made $25,000 from it. Of the 25 people who attended, 15 of them agreed to the $10,000 price he was charging for the annual membership. That was another $150,000 in sales that all came from the initial campaign.

What made this work so well was the initial list was super-targeted. These were all hand-chosen people he knew would be interested in this type of thing. The profit for each sale was high enough that it was easy to justify spending $45 per prospect just to put the offer in front of them.

In this case, he probably could not have made a better choice to market this particular product. The impact the video made was so impressive, I just couldn't help but want to be part of this group. Had he simply sent a flat letter, it would not have been nearly as impressive. That's what lumpy mail can do for you. It is one of the most powerful marketing strategies you can use.

But it is not right for every situation. Lumpy mail is much more effective when you have a very specific target audience, and you know your product can fulfill their need. In addition, your sales price has to be high enough to justify the cost of the lumpy mail.

What Is The Best Type Of Mail Piece To Use?

There is no right answer for this question. The best type of mail piece depends on what you're trying to do in your sales process. In many cases, using multiple different mail pieces is an effective strategy. Each mail piece has plusses and minuses given the situation. It's vital that you understand what you're doing, and how each type of mail piece could be used to get the best possible outcome.

I would like to point out some of the pros and cons of each of the five main types of mail pieces I have discussed.

POSTCARDS

Pros:

- They don't have to open a letter to see the message.
- Because you can see the message without opening an envelope, multiple mailings help build a brand or name recognition, even if they throw the postcards away without reading them.
- People often keep postcards for future use. They might keep a coupon for a special offer on the refrigerator.
- Postcards are the least expensive way to send out Direct Mail.

Cons:

- It is difficult to make a final sale with a postcard.
- It is difficult to make a complex sale with a postcard.

LETTERS

Pros:

- A very personal letter has a better chance of connecting with the recipient.

- Letters can be an effective tool for making final sales. Long letters often perform better than short letters.

- Letters have more time to tell a story.

Cons:

- Letters to have to be opened, so a poorly designed envelope may go straight into the trash before being read. People in a hurry don't always take time to open letters even if they are interested.

- If you use a strategy that tries to fool the prospect, they may get mad and throw letter in the trash anyway.

SELF-MAILERS

Pros:

- Self-Mailers can be very personal, giving you a better chance of connecting with the recipient.

- There is no need for an envelope, which makes them cost effective.

- They can do some really creative things that get attention.

Cons:

- These can get chewed up in the mail and are limited in space.

PRIORITY/SPECIAL DELIVERY MAIL

Pros:

- Priority/special delivery mail can be very effective in getting the recipient to pay attention to the mail piece.

- It gives you more room to include more materials.

Cons:

- This type of mail is more expensive than postcards and letters.
- It is usually more difficult to address and seal than letters or postcards.

LUMPY MAIL

Pros:

- Lumpy mail is the most effective mail piece in terms of getting noticed.
- It typically has a very high response rate.

Cons:

- It is the most expensive type of mail.
- Coming up with creative ideas is not always easy.
- Sourcing creative items is sometimes difficult.

Chapter 10

Sales Copy Can Make or Break You

Having effective sales copy is the second most important thing to success in any type of marketing, only preceded by going after the right target market.

In Direct Mail Marketing, copy tends to be more important than format or design. Don't get me wrong; effective formatting and design can accent the copy and help get your point across, but the copy itself is the most important thing. I'll give you some general rules for copywriting, and also talk specifically about different mail pieces and nuances of those mail pieces.

Probably the single most important thing you need to think about when writing copy is to put yourself in the position of the person receiving your offer, and ask this question after every statement: "Who cares?" The "who" is the prospect. If the prospect doesn't care about every single thing you say in your copy, don't say it. This is true of headlines, sub-headlines, body copy, offers, guarantees, and bonuses. When you write, you always have to be thinking in terms of benefits to the person reading it. You want to make the benefits so compelling that they just have to respond to your offer.

Postcard Copy Tips

It is difficult to make a sale from a postcard. Most postcards are used as lead generation tools. There's just not enough space in a postcard to tell a complete sales story in most cases. But they are an inexpensive lead generation tool that can be very effective.

Three rules for postcards:

1) Offer on front and back
2) Deadline on front and back
3) Personalize front and back

Offer on front and back:

When your prospect goes through their stack of mail, you have no control over which side of the postcard is up when they go through the stack. Remember, you only have the three seconds to get their attention, and chances are they're only going to look at the side that is showing when they pick it up. It is vital to have your main offer and headline on both sides of the postcard, so that no matter what side they see they will get the main message.

Deadline on front and back:

Another key element of effective copywriting is to have a deadline for response. For the same reasons I just mentioned, having the deadline on both sides is critical.

Personalize front and back:

It's a proven fact that the more you personalize a mailing, the more effective it is. Again, use their name and any other personalization you can add on both sides to give you the best possible chance to get their attention.

Sales Letter Copy Tips

Sales letters are typically contained in some sort of envelope. The envelope can be a regular business envelope, a large priority mail type of envelope, or some sort of lumpy mail packaging. In all cases, the job of the envelope is just to get someone to read the sales letter. The rest of this chapter is going to focus mainly on writing copy for sales letters. However, the same practices can be used for any sort of marketing, including postcards, print ads, and Online Marketing. Over the years, there have been many very successful campaigns that used a long sales letter in a newspaper or magazine.

Basic Roadmap of Good Sales Copy

Below is a very rough outline of the basic components of a sales letter. These don't necessarily have to be in this exact order, but it should be close. There are some nuances. For instance, you can talk about the guarantee in many different places, including the headline. In fact, the earlier you talk about it the better.

- **Headline**
- **Opening paragraph with benefits to reader - no more than three benefits.**
- **Credibility points**
- **Lifestyle connection**
- **Tell your story**
- **Lay out pain points to reader**

- **Tell more stories**
- **Make irresistible offer - solve pain problem with benefits**
- **Guarantee (can be anywhere)**
- **Deadlines and scarcity**
- **Bonuses**
- **Call to action**
- **Testimonials (can use throughout)**
- **Close and signature**
- **PS**
- **PPS**
- **PPPS (The more the better!)**

Headline

The headline is the most important part of the copy. A good headline will get you 80% of the way to a response. The chief job of the headline is to get the reader to read the rest of the copy. You have to draw them in with the headline.

Headlines answer the following issues:

- **So what?**
- **Who cares?**
- **What's in it for me?**
- **Why are you bothering me?**

You need to spend a lot of time coming up with the ideal headline. A good way to do it is to brainstorm 50 to 100 different versions. Headlines are a fairly formulaic process. If you research people who are using effective headlines, you can sort of get an idea as to what is effective and what is not. Don't hesitate to swipe other headlines and make minor changes that apply to your market. After you've brainstormed your list, go through it and decide which ones you think are best. Often your second and third choices can become the sub-headlines under your main headline.

Use the Dan Kennedy guide to test your headline.

1) Will it make the reader read the next sentence?

2) Will it stand alone? (If you ran the headline and just a phone number in an ad, would you get a response?)

Examples of Excellent Headlines:

Discover 7 Quick & Easy Formulas
for Writing Super-Responsive Classified Ads!

I'll Teach You How to Quickly & Easily
Get All the Credit You've Ever Wanted—100% Guaranteed.
Or I'll Pay You $50 for Wasting Your Time!

Discover the Simple, yet Little-Known Secrets
for Creating Your Own Best-Selling Information Product
in a Single Evening!

In Just 27 Minutes,
While Sitting in Your Most Comfortable Chair,
You'll Discover Everything You Need to Know
to Create Your Own Dynamite Website
that Brings in Cash Daily!

In Less Than 30 Days,
You'll Notice a Huge Improvement in Your Vocabulary
Using Our Simple Pocket Guide
for Only 5 Minutes a Day.
It's a Fast and Easy Way
to Make a Huge Difference in Your Life!

How to Give Yourself the Gift of Daily Inspiration
Quickly & Easily!

Your headline MUST contain a major part of your irresistible offer. It should be centered around your USP (Unique Selling Proposition).

Opening paragraph

Once you've written your headline and sub-headlines, the next stage is the opening paragraph. One huge mistake most people make is to immediately start talking about themselves in the opening paragraph. They start saying things like, "We have been in business for 50 years and we are located in a nice building…" Bad move.

You need to think back to what I said earlier about speaking the language of benefits to the prospect. Don't talk about yourself, talk about the prospect. Remember to ask the question, "Who cares?" after each line. The person who needs to care is the prospect.

You need to immediately start off with a benefit statement.

A good formula to use to help you with this process is the "if...then" formula. Using this formula will force you to start talking in terms of what will benefit the prospect. For example, "If you want to be extremely successful in your marketing, using the tips and techniques in this book will get you well on your way."

It is vitally important to remind the prospect why it is important for them to keep reading in the opening paragraph. Restate up to three benefits in the opening paragraph. No more than three.

Credibility Points

The next stage of effective copy is to establish your credibility. You need to prove to the prospect that you are worth listening to. Again, it's not about how long you've been in business and how nice your building is. It's about giving them a few key points to let them know you really do know what you're talking about.

Establish a lifestyle connection and personality

Use social proof to talk about your lifestyle. Don't overtly talk about your success. Instead, say something like, "I jumped on the plane with my son to go see the Super Bowl last week." It implies that you are successful and have a lot of money without outright saying it. Most people can relate to wanting to spend time with their family. It is important because it adds further reasons for a person to listen to you.

Tell Your Story

Telling a personal story about yourself is critical to successful bonding with the prospect. This may seem like it is in direct conflict with what I just said a minute ago about not talking about yourself. No one cares about the boring stuff that every business seems to talk about—good employees, good prices, nice building, etc. Telling a good story about yourself, designed to draw the reader in, is a good strategy. You need to put everything in terms that relate to the prospect.

An effective model for this is what we call the "hero's journey" model. Many movies follow this model with great success. You can use it in marketing as well.

Hero stories start out with the hero facing a problem, and enduring pain and hardship. Then the hero finds the answer to the problem, and with great sacrifice, ends up winning in the end, and living happily ever after. We can use that same model in our sales letters.

You start out talking about the hardship you had in the past. Focus a lot on the hardship and pain, especially those items that you know will relate to your prospects. Then you talk about the miracle breakthrough—the day you turned your life around.

Example:

> *I was driving in my car home from a job I hated. I was sweating like crazy after a crappy day at work. I had the windows down because it was hot out and I couldn't afford to fix my air conditioning. I missed my kids' sporting events because I worked so much. I hated my life.*

Then I came across a marketing system that would teach me to start my own business. I didn't even have enough money to buy the system. But I knew that successful people invested in themselves, and I wanted to be successful. So I used the last few hundred dollars of credit I had on my credit card to buy the system. Using that system completely turned my life around. Today I work out of my house on the beach. I don't miss any of my kid's games. I vacation in tropical places, have a great relationship with my wife and I'm happier than ever.

It is vital that the story relates to what you really do for your customers. If they can relate to your story, the obvious solution is to purchase your product.

It is important to get the prospect to relate to you as a person. You need them to relate to your pain and suffering. Think about the objections your customers might have when you're telling your story. Answer those objections as you tell the story.

Key Point: Copy must be entertaining. If you bore people you lose them.

Lay Out Pain Points

After you've told your story, which should contain a lot of pain, you can clearly lay out the pain points in summary fashion for the reader. Later you're going to solve those pain points. You want to get him or her thinking about it.

Tell More Stories

There is no better way to keep your copy entertaining and to illustrate points than to tell stories. Tell a story to illustrate each key benefit, pain point, and objection. The more stories you tell, the more you connect with the reader. Again, make sure to focus on pain and then solve the problem.

Lay out irresistible offer in detail

Here is where you lay it all out in a logical fashion for the reader to understand exactly what they're going to get. It must be in great detail, and focus on benefits to the reader. If you can monetize those benefits, it is even better. In other words, tell them the value of each service. Use the full retail value when you're doing this. The higher the number, the better. Then, at the end, give them an overall package price that is far cheaper than the individual items.

Bonuses

Always use bonuses. It has been proven that adding bonuses increases response rates.

A bonus is exactly what you might think it is. It is something extra that you give the person when they respond. A rule of thumb is the more bonuses, the better. It is not uncommon for the list of bonuses to be longer than the list of benefits from the main offer. Make sure you monetize the bonuses as well. The larger the numbers, the better. We all like to get things for free, even wealthy people.

Free reports are the most common bonuses you see, especially in information marketing. Think about all the things you do for your customers, and if possible, package up some of those benefits into bonus packages.

Another effective strategy is to add a list of bonus choices, from which the prospect can choose which one he/she wants.

This changes the thinking from *Yes or no* to *Which bonus do I want?*

Always Use Guarantees

Any guarantee is extremely important to removing risk in the mind of the prospect. If you can't guarantee 100% satisfaction, figure out what you can guarantee and list it.

If you can't guarantee what you sell, find something else to sell! Everyone can find a way to guarantee something. Don't be afraid of guarantees.

Many people are afraid to give 100% satisfaction guarantees because they are afraid dishonest people will take advantage of them. Yes, occasionally there is a dishonest person who's looking to get something for nothing and will try to take advantage of you. That is a fact of life. However, that is a small percentage, and a very small price to pay for the dramatic increase in sales you'll get by guaranteeing your product or services.

Three Main Types Of Guarantees

1) **Satisfaction** - If you're not satisfied we will give you back your money.

2) **Results** - If you don't get a certain result with the product or service we sell to you, we will give you back your money.

3) **Perception** - this is something that enhances the positive perception of you and your offer. "We promise to answer the phone with a smile on our face" is a perception guarantee.

More Guarantees Are Better

When displaying a guarantee, make a big deal about it in your marketing materials. Put a box around it and make it look special. Do not bury it in the end; show it right up front. Including the guarantee in the headline is also a good strategy.

Guarantee in the headline:
"I will sell your house in 90 days or I'll buy it, guaranteed!"

"If your friends don't accuse you of having a facelift, return the empty jar and will give you all your money back!"

Name Your Guarantees

Just like naming your offers, naming a guarantee will make it more memorable. The examples below are from copywriting guru Bill Glaser.

My personal, make you happy guarantee

I guarantee this will be the most valuable event ever having to do with making really big money in the retail industry.

My personal, super strength guarantee

I guarantee that this will be the biggest, baddest, most valuable seminar ever having to do with making really big, fast cash, in the mortgage industry.

Deadlines and Scarcity are Critical

There is no offer without a deadline. People are famous for procrastinating. Even good intentions will often get lost at the bottom of the pile if there is not a deadline.

Plus, the deadline builds up the importance of the offer. If it is so great, there should be a limited supply. The deadline helps to promote the limited supply.

Testimonials

Testimonials are perhaps the most powerful tool you have in your arsenal. What other people say about you is much more believable than what you say about yourself. You need to use testimonials as much as you possibly can. You can never have too many.

Written testimonials are good. Audio or video testimonials are even better.

You can use them at any point in the sales copy. They can be part of the headline, interspersed in callout boxes, on the back of the sales letter, on a completely separate sheet.

Two Major Kinds Of Testimonials

Outcome-driven Testimonial:

What is the outcome the person got from using your product or service?

Example:

"I received a 3% response for my mailings and was able to close 2 deals, which earned me $35,000 in profit. This is the best thing I have ever done!"

Overcoming Objections Testimonial:

These types of testimonials answer the objections that your typical prospects have. The best way to do this is to make a list of all the reasons people don't buy from you, then find testimonials that answer those objections.

One technique you can use to get testimonials written exactly the way you want them is to write them yourself, and get your customers to approve them. You will find that almost 100% of the time the customers will approve exactly what you've written. Of course this assumes they like you, so obviously you need to go to your best customers to utilize the strategy.

Don't Use Blind Testimonials.

Don't use partial names. The more information you can put about the person giving the testimonial, the better. Your goal is to prove it is from a real person.

Asking for testimonials is a normal course of business. When you do something good for someone and you know they're happy, ask them to take a moment and write that down and send it to you.

Contests are another good way to get testimonials. Send out a letter or email to all your clients, and ask them for testimonials in exchange for some reward. You can enter them all into a drawing for a prize of some sort. You'll be amazed at how easy it is to get people to respond to this.

Always get permission to use the testimonials. The best way to do this is at the time you're asking for the testimonial. People never say no, but it's still a good idea to ask.

Don't use the word "testimonials" in your marketing. Use words like "What clients say about us," or "What people have to say."

Call To Action

So many people miss this point when they create their marketing materials. They will list their contact information, but they don't specifically say what they want the reader to do. Spell it out in detail. It may sound dumb, but if you don't tell the reader exactly what to do, they often will not do anything, even if they are interested.

Call 800-xxx-xxxx within 48 hours!

Go to our webpage at www.callme.com
and register today for your free gift.

Close and Signature

It may not seem like a big deal, but if this is a personal letter, you need to sign it like you are signing a personal letter. Use your full name and signature. If you are going for the true personal letter look, it is a good idea to sign in blue ink.

The P.S.

The P.S. is the second most read part of a sales letter online or offline.

Why? Because people have been trained to know that all of the goodies are in the P.S.

The P.S. needs to include at least one of the following:

- **Restatement of the benefits**
- **Introduce a new benefit**
- **Restate the promise**
- **Introduce a new promise**
- **Provide credibility**
- **Indicate urgency or a deadline**
- **Restate the guarantee**
- **Expand on the guarantee**
- **Restate the bonuses**
- **Restate the discounts**

The more the better.

Other Tips

Name Your Offer

An offer is more effective and memorable if it has a name. Something like the "Super Duper Carpet Cleaning Deal" is more memorable than just "Cheap Carpet Cleaning."

Create a "Hate" List

When writing copy, create a list of things the prospect hates, and then answer those objections.

Build Value

Break down your offer into parts. Show the value of each portion of the offer so it collectively sounds like a lot more than just one statement.

Give Payment Options

Adding payment options will typically increase response. Allow the clients to make multiple payments over time, or offer a cash discount if they pay up front.

Apples to Oranges Comparison

Always compare your offer to something else in order to build value. An example for a real estate business might be something like: "If you were to get a professional appraisal, it would cost you between $300 and $500. I will give you a market evaluation, free."

Add a deluxe offer to your choices.

If you have a membership program, have the ultra-deluxe membership that costs twice as much. If you are a tanning company, have a package that is two to three times more expensive. It might be "Unlimited Tans" Typically, at least 20% of the people will choose a deluxe offer.

Copy Length

The single most asked question in the copywriting business is "What is better, long copy or short copy?" People tend to think that if it's too long, no one will read it, especially in our fast-paced cell phone and Internet society.

It's not the length of the sales letter that determines whether or not they will read it. What matters is if they are interested in what you have to say. **If you bore them, they absolutely will not read it!**

If someone is interested in what you've got to say, they will read on forever.

The key is to find the right person, who has the best chance of being interested, and draw that person in with compelling headlines and a very interesting copy.

Dual Readership Path

A dual readership path describes a method of writing that will allow you to reach different types of readers.

There are four main types of readers.

1) Scan-man or Lady-Scan: Will scan only the headlines and never go back and read the details.

2) Detail Dude or Detail Darla: Will read the details top to bottom, headlines and all.

3) Mr. or Ms. Efficient: Will scan the headlines first, and if they're interested, read the details.

4) Timmy or Tina Trash: Won't read anything and are quick to use the round file.

When you use a dual readership path, you will highlight headlines, bullet points and callouts. The reader should be able to understand the offer after reading only those items.

By writing in this manner, you have a chance to grab the attention of Scan Man, Lady Scan, or Mr. or Ms. Efficient. Detail Dude and Detail Darla will read everything anyway, so you get them as well. There's nothing you can do for Timmy or Tina trash, so don't worry about them.

Even the detail people sometimes scan first. It is almost human nature to quickly scan material to see if it holds our interest. If you write effectively, you can grab most people's attention during that scan.

Graphic/Cosmetic Enhancements

Graphic/Cosmetic enhancements are almost as important as the copy itself. They will increase the likelihood of readership, and help guide the reader to the important points. I mentioned earlier you have to be interesting. Cosmetic enhancements help to make things interesting.

Benefits of cosmetic enhancements:

- **Keep the person reading**
- **Highlight the key points**
- **Make long copy seem less intimidating**
- **Relay your message by just reading the cosmetic information (dual readership path)**

Types of Graphic/Cosmetic Enhancements:

- **Boldface**
- **Underlining**
- **Large fonts**
- **Indenting**
- **Subheads**
- **Screens**
- **Shading**
- **Handwritten notes**
- **Cross-outs**
- **Highlighting**
- **Sidebars**
- **Photos**

What I'm not saying is to turn it into a graphic design masterpiece. Cosmetic enhancements are one thing. Turning it into nothing but a bunch of images, photos and graphics will often distract from the message.

Often when you turn a sales letter over to a graphic designer, they will turn an effective piece into a piece that doesn't pull at all. They get hung up on the graphics and minimize the importance of the words.

The main thing is you are trying to get a person to read your copy and get the message you're trying to send. If your graphic enhancements take away from that, they are not going to help. Use them, but don't overdo it.

Biggest Mistakes in Copywriting

1) Leaving out personal story
2) No USB or good headline
3) No guarantees or guarantee not up front
4) No testimonials
5) Looks and sounds boring
6) No call to action

It is important to focus on the prospect or customer for the key elements of any marketing material. The key elements are the headline, the offer, the call to action, the benefits, the guarantees, and the postscript (PS).

But in between, you need to develop compelling copy that draws the reader in, establishes credibility, and enhances their chance of saying yes to your offer. Your goal is to connect you to the reader in a way that makes him or her relate to you as a human being. You want your readers to feel you are walking in their shoes. Stories make you credible. They establish you as a resource they should respect and want to do business with.

I want to spend a little bit more time on the personal story, because that is probably the single biggest mistake people make.

Why is a story important? Because that's how we are raised. Growing up, our parents read us stories. Our society likes stories.

The challenge is to work in the story at the right time. You should tell your story in every sales letter you write. And by the way, make sure it is a compelling story. Don't tell them your entire life story and all the boring details. Focus on the items that build interest in the product you sell. Use the "hero story" format discussed earlier.

For instance, as a real estate investor, you might say something like:

> "I grew up poor and had no money. I attended my first real estate seminar when I was 23 years old and in debt up to my ears. At the end of that weekend I thought my head was going to explode with all the information and I wasn't sure where to start. I was scared to death. So I went back to the beginning, and step-by-step did exactly what I was taught.
>
> Fast-forward to 10 years later.
>
> I still use some of those early techniques I learned at that seminar, and I have built a real estate empire of over 100 properties in my portfolio. We flip 15 properties every single month. I have reached a lifestyle beyond my wildest dreams. I spend more time with my children and wife, take more vacations, and have a larger bank account than I ever dreamed possible.
>
> I've taken everything I've learned over the last 10 years and packaged it up in this one super program. I'm going to teach you how to do exactly what I did and achieve the same success."

That is a story that a potential real estate investor would be interested in hearing. It establishes interest, credibility, and lets the reader know they are just like you. You'll notice at the beginning of this book I told my story. Hopefully it helped you to realize that you too can be successful in marketing if you just put your mind to it. If I can do it, anyone can do it.

Once you have a story, tell it every time. Use it in all your marketing materials were space permits. That doesn't mean it has to be in every single piece, but it should appear at least once as part of the sales process.

Effective marketing is all about effective communication and getting inside the head of the readers to motivate them to do what you want them to do. And you want them to feel good about doing it.

Insider Strategies To Increase Your Direct Mail Response

Personalization increases response by 30%. People respond much better to their name. Use their name as often as you can.

PHOTOGRAPHS

The best photographs relay a story. Use photos that will appeal to your target market. Photos that reinforce the content or tone of your message will work to make that message more memorable.

GRABBERS

Grabbers are things either in the envelope or attached to the envelope that get people's attention. Lumpy mail sort of falls into the grabber category. Adding a small premium is a grabber. A good example of a grabber is a small wooden token called "Round TUIT." It is basically a piece of wood about the size of a half dollar that has the word "TUIT" printed on it. The copy relates to getting "Around to it." It is a funny grabber that almost always increases response. Grabbers usually pay for themselves.

INVOLVEMENT

Anything interactive is an Involvement. Watching a video can be considered Involvement. Asking someone to take a sticker and peel off one part and put it on another part is Involvement. Another strategy might be to include a pen in your mailing, along with a list of things they have to check off that lead them to your offer. If you can get people checking boxes on your page, you have a very good chance of getting them to buy from you. Busy fingers increase response rates.

PREMIUMS

A premium is a gift for responding. It can be offered as a free gift, or sometimes for a small charge. Premiums typically increase response by about 30%.

LIVE STAMPS

Live stamps increase response over preprinted postal indicia. (Indicia are postal markings used in many standard mail or bulk mail applications instead of stamps.) Crooked or upside down stamps do better than straight stamps. Multiple stamps do better than single stamps.

HANDWRITTEN FONTS

Handwritten fonts almost always increase response rates over typed fonts, especially when using the strategy of trying to write a personal letter. It can even be effective on self-mailers and postcards.

You can actually handwrite the letters if you like, but that is extremely time-consuming. There are services who will do actual handwritten letters for you, but that is expensive. In today's world, most mail houses have the ability to use handwritten fonts on their printers, which look very realistic and are more cost-effective.

FIRST-CLASS MAIL VERSUS STANDARD OR BULK MAIL

The main difference between first-class and bulk mail is price. In general, first-class costs around $.20 more per piece than standard mail for most letter or large postcard mailings. The post office gives you a discount in exchange for allowing them to take more time to deliver the piece. Standard mail can take anywhere from 1 to 4 weeks to be delivered, depending on how far away the delivery point is from the mail drop.

If time is of the essence, use first-class. You just don't have enough control over delivery times using standard mail.

In general, first-class mail, using live stamps, will pull better than standard, or bulk mail. Stamps, first-class or standard, will pull better than preprinted indicia.

However, there are exceptions. If you're sending postcards, or other obvious mail pieces that are clearly marketing materials, it is not really necessary to use first-class stamps. No one is going to confuse a marketing postcard with a personal letter; you might as well save the postage and send it out standard mail. That is, of course, if you are in no hurry. If your offer is time critical, you may want to spend the money for first-class anyway just to ensure it gets there on time.

If you're sending a letter, stamps are almost always the preferred method for the best response rates. However, many direct-mail companies, including ours, have ways to use standard mail stamps along with a cancellation that looks like a first-class cancellation that gives the impression of first-class stamps. We have tested this side-by-side with first-class stamps and have not seen any difference in response.

Chapter 11

Systems + Systems + Systems = Success

At this point, you might be thinking to yourself "this sounds great, but it also sounds overwhelming." The way to overcome that feeling is to systemize everything.

These are the things you should have in place

- Systems to identify potential prospects
- Systems to make sure you collect information on all your prospects and customers so you can properly follow up
- A database where you can store and easily retrieve that information
- An email system that allows you to automatically send out messages to both prospects and customers
- Separate marketing systems to handle prospects and customers (they should not be approached the same way)

- **Systems to remind yourself to do regular marketing**

- **Systems to ensure that regular marketing goes out on time each month**

- **Systems in place so that all of your employees know exactly what to do, and when key employees are gone, other employees can step in and make sure the work gets done properly**

- **Systems to make sure the customers feel important every time they contact your company**

Every one of these systems is vital to the success of your marketing program. If you don't have a system, it you'll inevitably drop the ball, which will ultimately cost you money. You may not see it right away, but I guarantee you'll hurt yourself when you try to fly by the seat of your pants.

For a marketing system to be successful it has to be regular and predictable. To be predictable, mailings and advertisements have to go out on a regular basis, and you have to know what type of results you can expect from each of your campaigns in advance. The best way to know this is to have systems to make sure things get out on time, systems to track results, and systems to follow up and make changes.

Read the next chapter for an exciting system that will put all this together and blow your mind.

Chapter 12

Ultimate
Direct Marketing Strategy

Direct Mail + Online Automatic Tracking + Online Remarketing + Offline Direct Mail = Massive Success

By now you should have concluded that Direct Mail is not dead. It is clear from this book that not only is it not dead, it is still a vital piece of a comprehensive and successful marketing program. But it's just a piece.

Granted, you can build an entire marketing program around Direct Mail by itself. Even with today's society, you can still do it that way. And there are plenty of companies that have success doing that.

But if you really want to accelerate and optimize your marketing, combine both offline direct marketing techniques and online systems for maximum results.

Now it is time to put all this together.

Just to review, I have talked about the basic core principles of successful marketing. I've talked about creating your USP, and an irresistible offer.

I've explained the fundamentals of Direct Response, specifically Direct Mail Marketing.

I've talked about the different types of Direct Mail and the best practices.

I discussed how to use Direct Mail to drive online traffic, and how to follow up with people using online tools.

I've talked about copywriting, how to write headlines, integrate your story, and make irresistible offers. I talked about the use of guarantees, and deadlines, and scarcity. I explained how to craft your P.S.

I have also talked about the importance of frequency and follow-up with both prospects and customers.

It probably seems a bit overwhelming. Let me try to boil it down into a very simple strategy.

Because different people respond in different ways to offers, the most effective overall marketing system is to combine both online and offline tactics.

Most small businesses cannot afford to do radio or TV advertising, so Direct Mail and space advertising become the most logical offline methods to use. (Space advertising is any type of advertising you do in magazines or newspapers.)

Here is the ultimate strategy. I am going to assume you've already identified your ideal prospect, you know your USP, and you have an irresistible offer.

Ultimate System to Generate New Prospects

❏ **Purchase List:** Purchase a targeted mailing list. This one is pretty straightforward. Make sure it's a list of your ideal prospects based on your ideal customer.

❏ **Create Direct Mail Campaign:** Create a three or four step Direct Mail campaign using postcards, letters or lumpy mail. You can use a combination if you like. What you use is not important as long as the pieces contain all the essential elements discussed in this book. What is important is that this campaign flows from one piece to the next. I talked about repetition earlier. For best results, you want to do at least a three step campaign, and if your budget will allow, even more. Your entire goal is to entice the person to respond with interest by either making a small initial purchase or asking for more information.

❏ **Offer a tracking phone number and URL for your landing page:** Your Direct Mail campaign will have at least two methods of responding. It will contain a phone number and a URL to a landing page online. Make sure you use a unique phone number and landing page for each campaign. Creating a landing page is very simple, and there are multiple software programs that can easily do this for you. You do not need to have a comprehensive website to have a simple landing page.

❏ **Have a system that will track your mail through the U.S. Postal Service.** This is especially important if you're using standard mail. It can take up to four weeks for standard mail to be delivered, and you need to know when it's going to hit so you can be prepared for the incoming increase in call volume. These systems are relatively new, and there are only a few printers who offer them. We at Graphic Connections Group have the ability to do this for you.

❏ **Track phone calls and visits to your landing page with an automated system:** The system will also have a tracking mechanism that logs and records all phone calls. When people go to the landing page, that activity is recorded as well. It is important that you are able to track how many people go to the landing page, even if they do not opt in to the page. Tracking is vital to measuring success in any marketing program.

Just about everyone fails to track the results effectively. To avoid this problem, make sure you have a system in place that automates this process. The ideal situation is a system with an online portal that will show you the progress of the mail traveling to the post office, so you know exactly when it hits.

The second part is to show how many people call the phone number that's listed on the mail piece. It is a good idea to use a separate tracking phone number for each campaign. Your system should be able to do this. At Graphic Connections Group, we have such a system, and offer it to those clients who mail with us.

The third system is to measure how many people go to the webpage and at least consider opting in. You'll know if they respond when they opt in, but you also need to know if they at least went to the webpage. That will tell you if your sales material was effective in getting their interest.

❏ **Offer either free information, or a minimal purchase as a first step:** It is typically best, especially if your product or service is more than $100, to use a two-step approach to marketing. The first step is just to get the lead to respond with interest in your product. You can offer something for free in exchange for them calling or opting into your landing page, or you can sell something for under $100 as an initial purchase. To maximize leads, you're typically better off offering something for free.

❏ **Remarket using retargeting ads:** This system will add cookies to their computer, and re-targeting ads will appear in front of them for your product or service over the next few months when they go to other websites. Then re-target every person that goes the landing page. What makes it extremely powerful is you are giving yourself a better chance to get someone's attention with your Direct Mail piece. If you can at least get them to go to your landing page, even if they don't opt in, they will be hit multiple times with re-target ads in the future. Hopefully after seeing your ads pop up over and over, they will eventually click through and take advantage of your offer.

❑ **Mail a "Shock-and-Awe" kit to people who respond to your offer:** A "shock and awe" package is basically a box or thick envelope of materials that is so impressive, the recipient is shocked and awed. What you put in this package is up to you, but at a minimum, it should have the item they were promised, plus a longer sales letter enticing them to take advantage of the larger purchase, and a newsletter, book, or CD that shows you are an expert in your field. You might also throw in some additional free gifts just to get their attention. Remember, you're trying to stand out from the crowd. Very few of your competitors will send them anything like this. The "shock and awe" kit alone will get the prospect's attention.

❑ **Send the auto-responder email series to every person who responds to your offer:** We are not abandoning online tactics. The auto-responder series is still a very effective tool. You can't send too many emails, as long as the emails are interesting and valuable. I recommend at least a series of 10 to start, being sent at least every other day for the first couple weeks. As time goes on, continue to add to the series and expand as large as you can. The goal of the auto-responder series is to establish your expertise, and also encourage the person to take advantage of your larger offer.

❏ **Mail via USPS, as well as email, a regular monthly newsletter to every person who has responded to your offer (take them offline):** I mentioned earlier that taking your prospects and customers offline is an effective way to build a stronger relationship and increase sales. The sooner you can take that relationship offline, the stronger your relationships and sales will be. Again, I am not suggesting you abandon online tactics like auto-responders. I'm simply suggesting that taking someone offline in addition to using the online tactics is extremely effective.

❏ **Calculate your results using your online tracking system, adjust and mail again:** Your online mail tracking system will provide you with detailed numbers of how many people placed calls, visited your website, and how many re-targeting ads each of those people saw. You also have recordings of the phone calls you can use to evaluate whether your people are answering the phones and handling the calls properly. Use that data to make your system better. Now that you have exact tracking statistics, you can decide if your mail piece was successful or not. You can also use that to compare the next mail piece. The goal of all marketing is to continually improve your results, but you can't do that if you don't look at the statistics each time.

There you have it! What I have described here is a system that will put you light years ahead of your competition. Most of your competition has a hard enough time even sending out an occasional marketing piece. Fewer than 10% have any sort of comprehensive and organized system anywhere near what I've described. Less than 1% will have the online tracking system I described, because this technology is brand-new. There are very few mail houses in the country that offer this type of technology.

We at Graphic Connections Group have this technology, and are using it every day. Using offline Direct Mail systems to drive online traffic, using the retargeting technology to stay in front of them, and hitting them with both online and offline marketing messages, is an absolute winning strategy.

Is it a lot of work? Yes, of course it is. But anything worthwhile usually is. Once you get this set up the first time, it is not difficult to manage it. Once you have a winning formula, all you have to do is repeat that formula over and over again until it stops working. Then you adjust and begin again. You'll still use the same system; you just need to tweak your marketing pieces occasionally to keep it fresh.

Chapter 13

What Next?

The Answer Depends On Where You Are Today

If your business is not where you wanted it to be, you need to sit down and take a hard look at your business. The first thing you need to do is assess where you stand today. It can't move forward until you know where you are. A completely comprehensive marketing system is a large undertaking. You may already have part of the critical elements in place. Start with the personal assessment.

Below is a checklist to use for this purpose. Once you assess where you are today, you can decide where to go from here.

❏ **Do you have a steady flow of leads?**

❏ **Do you know exactly how much business you will do next week, next month, or next year?**

❏ **Do you have a plan to grow even when the economy is down?**

❏ **Do you want to grow?**

- ❏ Do you have a system to replace the natural attrition that happens with every business?

- ❏ Do you have a website?

- ❏ Do you have a unique selling proposition (USP)?

- ❏ How do you introduce your product to new prospects?

- ❏ Do you have outside sales people?

- ❏ You have inside sales people?

- ❏ Are you a retail location?

- ❏ Does your product or service offer repeat business or one-time sales?

- ❏ Do you have existing customers?

- ❏ Do you have a database with information about all your existing customers?

- ❏ Have you identified your ideal customer, and their characteristics?

- ❏ How much revenue and profit comes from a typical sale?

- ❏ What is the lifetime value of a customer?

- ❏ How often do repeat customers order from you?

- ❏ Do you use any sort of advertising or Direct Response Marketing now?

- ❏ Do you have existing sales copy already written?

❏ Do you have a marketing budget?

❏ Do you know how much it costs you in advertising and marketing to obtain a new customer?

❏ Do you have any experience in Direct Mail Marketing or advertising?

❏ Are you a writer?

❏ Are you willing to learn how to write copy yourself? If not, are you willing to pay someone else to do it?

❏ Do you have a current prospect list with names addresses, phone numbers and emails?

❏ Do you guarantee your products?

❏ Do you have an auto-responder such as Constant Contact or AWeber?

❏ Do you have a CRM system such as Salesforce, or Infusionsoft?

❏ Do you publish a newsletter?

❏ Do you have a blog on your website? Do you post to it?

❏ Do you use social media in your marketing?

❏ Do you use radio, or TV, or print advertising?

❏ Do you have a system in place to track results from mailings and advertisements?

❏ Have you ever used online advertising such as pay-per click, banner ads, or re-marketing?

Once you've done the self-assessment, look at the elements you do not have in place and decide what you think will give you the biggest bang for your buck in the shortest possible time.

Then Get To Work!

This can be a daunting task for many business owners. It can be so overwhelming that they don't know where to start, so they do nothing. If this sounds like you, I recommend hiring a marketing consultant to help you through this process.

Or, you can find a direct marketing company who has the expertise in helping you to craft your entire program, and work with them. My company, Graphic Connections Group, does just that. We can take you from where you are today to a completely comprehensive program, no matter how far away you are today.

You May Just Need A Few Tweaks - You May Need It All

Give us a call today at 636-519-8320, or go to www.gcfrog. com/info and fill out the form requesting more information.

We would love to help you on your journey to marketing prominence in your industry.

Chapter 14

Bonus Ideas

This last chapter is just a compilation of a bunch of miscellaneous ideas that might help you. Enjoy!

Thanksgiving Card Strategy

If you are sending out holiday or Christmas cards during December, stop doing it. Not because I have anything against Christmas for the holidays. In fact, I love Christmas. However, most companies send out cards during that time period, and because there are so many, your card could get lost in the shuffle.

Rather than do it at Christmas, why not send out a card at Thanksgiving? Thanksgiving is the time for giving thanks anyway, so it makes sense to thank your customers during that time. And very few people, if any, are sending cards at that time, so yours will get noticed. It is an excellent goodwill gesture.

Kick it up a notch: In addition to sending the Thanksgiving card, put a sealed envelope inside the card that says on the outside, "Please open this only after you finish displaying your Thanksgiving card."

People's natural curiosity will get them to open that envelope right away to see what's in it. Put some sort of an offer inside that envelope.

Use Swipe Files

A swipe file is a file you keep of examples of ads, sales letters, and marketing pieces from other people in all types of industries that you think are good. Simply save them in a file, and when it is time for you to create a marketing piece, refer to that file for ideas. There's no point in reinventing the wheel. Caution - do not blatantly plagiarize anything. Using swipe files for ideas is great but make sure you change them enough to make them original to you.

Keep rewriting copy of campaigns already written. If you have something that's working well, rewrite it slightly differently.

Borrow Ideas From Other Industries

Who's got stuff that's really working? It doesn't matter if it's not in your industry. If something is working in another industry, figure out how to use the same concept in your business, and deploy it.

Turn Ads Into Letters, Letters Into Postcards

There is no need to continually reinvent the wheel. Once you have a marketing message, using that same message reformatted in different pieces is smart and memorable.

Q&A Format For Quick Sales Letters

One way to crank out a quick message is to use the Q&A format. Write down the top 6 to 10 questions you know your customers have, and then answer the questions. It's simple.

Record The Presentation Of Someone Who Sells A Product Or Service Really Well

Find a top salesperson in your industry, and see if you can record one of their sales presentations. Use what they say in your copy. Since they are successful, you'll probably learn things you'll never hear anywhere else. They can be very powerful.

Do Joint Venture Deals

One of the most powerful ways you can get introduced to potential customers is to find someone else you trust and respect who is selling a product to the same types of people who fit your ideal profile. Make a deal with them to market each other's products to your own lists. Exactly how this deal is structured is up to your imagination.

Information marketers are especially adept at doing this. I will use this book as an example, since I am primarily a direct-mail guy. It would make sense for me to go to people who are primarily Internet marketers, and offer to sell their products to my customers, and get them to sell my products to their customers. Then work out some sort of revenue-sharing formula, and you both win.

Share Lists - Affiliate Marketing

Sharing lists and affiliate marketing are very similar to the previous section about joint venture deals. The only difference is how you handle it. Typically when you share lists, you might just make an agreement to trade your list with someone else and that's the end of it. It is still a good deal for two people in noncompeting but complementary markets.

Affiliate marketing typically involves giving an affiliate the link to your website, and they will market your products to their list, in a completely hands-off fashion. All they are doing is sending an email to their list, recommending you, and asking the recipients to click on a link which takes them to your website. That link has tracking codes in it so you will get your affiliate commission properly.

Affiliate marketing is an extremely powerful way to dramatically increase sales almost overnight. If you can find a person who has a very large email list, you'll be amazed at what can happen with one email.

Referral Marketing

Referral marketing is something I should've mentioned earlier, as it is probably one of the most effective ways that just about any business can increase sales without having a huge and complicated marketing system in place. It boils down to encouraging your customers to give you referrals at the time they are the happiest in your transaction. This usually occurs right after the sale is made.

There are a lot of different ways to do this, but the essence is to ask a person for referral and reward them when they give you one. Make it easy for them to refer you by offering some sort of introductory offer to the person they're referring. People who are referring you want to look good in the eyes of the people they're talking to. By giving them a special deal to offer, it's going to make them look like are doing their friends a favor.

Every single person who buys from you and has a good experience should be encouraged to give you referrals in a nonthreatening and easy way.

One very simple way is to include a "Shock-and-Awe" referral box with every order that is fulfilled. If it's something you hand-deliver, you can hand-deliver the referral box as well. If your business involves you shipping orders to people, it's very simple to attach an additional box or envelope to the side of the same shipping container for almost no extra money.

Don't Let Your Letters Or Designs Get Stagnant

When mailing to customers or prospects you have already spoken to, you need to mix things up a bit. Sending the same designs over and over to customers is fine for a while but soon it will cause them to lose interest.

Your mailings should be attention-grabbing and informative, not stale and boring. If you recently started offering a new service, a postcard letting your database know about it would be a smart move. The main point is to keep your company in the front of their mind and to keep them reading your postcards.

If you send the same cards to your customer database and your customers lose interest, you are wasting your money on postage. Your postcards won't get the attention you want.

Collect All The Information You Can From Your Customers And Prospects

It sounds like a no-brainer, but you would be surprised by how many companies fail to collect key client data. Names, addresses, phone numbers, emails, and even birthdays can be very useful.

It's not a bad idea to log the date they became a customer, and then use that in an anniversary mailing at some point in the future. Of course that's the anniversary of the day they became a customer, not their wedding anniversary.

Spell Your Clients' Names Correctly

Getting people's names wrong is like punching them in the face. No one likes to see their name spelled incorrectly. Take the time to make sure you get this right.

Don't Treat Your Customers Like Prospects

While form letters and generic emails may be easier for you, don't make the costly mistake of treating your customers like prospects. Have different letters and email sequences for customers and prospects. Once a prospect has moved into the customer field, stop sending them prospect mail.

Become An Expert In Your Field - Write A Book

There is no quicker way to claim expert status on any topic, than to write a book. There's something magical about putting ink on paper in the form of a written book. We equate books with the concept of reliable information. Our society has a high regard for authors. Writing a book is a huge undertaking, and it garners respect.

That may seem like an overwhelming task. It doesn't have to be. You just need to sit down and make some notes on topics that you know a lot about. Then put it in an outline form. Then systematically pick one topic at a time and write. If you are disciplined, you will be amazed at how you can make fast progress.

Let me first say that it helps to actually be an expert. I will use this book as an example. I have been studying marketing and Direct Mail for over 25 years. I know it backwards and forwards. So for me, all I had to do was create an outline of topics, then a few subtopics under each main topic, and I was ready to go. I did some research on some areas where I thought I needed more depth. I then organized it in a way that makes sense and is helpful to the reader.

Since I am a lousy typist, I spoke my thoughts into a microphone using voice recognition software, about each topic and subtopic.

I went through all the topics initially in what I will call "rough draft" form. I then went back a second time and did some editing, and organizing my thoughts. At that point, I added subtracted and organized.

I then passed the book onto an editor, and had that person do a rough edit, and rough proofread.

They gave me the book back, and I went through it again, page by page, editing it myself.

I handed it back to the editor a second time, then went through it one last time myself. Lastly, I turned it over to my in-house book designer and layout artist to turn it into a professional presentation. The entire project was done in about 8 weeks.

I now have a printed document that I am proud of, that I can use as a free gift, and also to establish credibility. Plus the entire process gave me several more ideas for other books and reports.

Test! Test! Test!

This is the one area where many marketers fall down. They think that they know everything there is to know about their prospects, and how they think. They think they can write copy and then just roll it out without a test. I cannot stress enough, that no matter how much you think you know about your customer, and how much you think an offer is going to work, do not bet the farm on any campaign until you test it first.

For a test to be statistically valid, you need at least 5000 pieces of mail. Unfortunately, a lot of marketers either cannot afford to mail 5000, or don't have a list that large.

So my recommendation is whatever the size of your list, break it down into at least three parts. Mail no more than one third of the list first time around as a test. Then evaluate the results, and go from there.

Once you establish a successful mail piece, keep using it until you're able to find another mail piece that is more successful. What that means is do side-by-side testing, comparing the successful piece against the new piece. If the new piece pulls better, it can then become your standard mailer. If it does not pull better, tweak it and try again. Never abandon a successful mail piece until you have something that is proven to pull better. Once you've established acceptable results from your primary mail piece, then you can mail to your entire list.

Chapter 15

Good is Good Enough

Marketing can be an overwhelming task. People can spend weeks and months, even years, trying to perfect a marketing campaign, thinking it has to be perfect before they release it. The problem is, it'll never be perfect. You don't know what works and doesn't work until you release it. So do your best the first time around, and get it out. You can make adjustments it from there.

I am constantly writing new sales letters and marketing campaigns. I do spend a lot of time trying to get each letter perfect. I will often write a letter, put it down for a couple of days, come back and change it all around. That is good for a couple of rounds. But at some point, you have got to send it out. I limit myself to no more than 3 rounds of edits and I go.

It's not always perfect. Sometime there are typos. On one hand you could say it makes me look bad if someone notices a typo. That is true. I might even lose a sale or two because of it. But how many sales did I lose by not mailing at all? Every day you delay costs to money.

If something is working, over time, my clients will point out mistakes and we will fix them and move on. Continuous improvement is a healthy process. Good is Good Enough. Get it out!

Chapter 16

Putting it all Together

We've gone over a lot of concepts in this book. Hopefully by now, you understand that Direct Response Marketing is one of the most powerful things you can do for any business, but especially for a small business. As you think about what you have read, keep the following points in mind: Direct Mail Marketing is a key element of Direct Response Marketing; Combining Direct Mail Marketing with Online Marketing is an extremely powerful combination.

They say what comes around goes around, or history repeats itself. That is certainly true for Direct Mail. Although Direct Mail has never completely gone out of style, there's no question that when the Internet boom first hit, the numbers declined. But marketers at all levels are starting to realize that good, old-fashioned, Direct Mail Marketing is an extremely powerful tool. Just look at your mailbox at home, and that should tell you how popular it is.

Successful businesses don't continue to do *anything* that doesn't work!

The reason it is so powerful is very basic. With it, you can target your ideal prospect. You can craft a multi-step campaign in such a way that you appeal to your ideal prospects' needs and desires. You can easily measure the results. It is something tangible. Exposure rate is much higher than any other type of marketing, because people still go to the mailbox, pick up their mail, and sort through it one piece at a time. There is no other marketing medium the offers that level of attention.

Marketing boils down to some very basic concepts. You have to first identify a pool of prospects. You then have to put a marketing message in front of that pool of prospects often enough, that when it finally comes time for them to be interested in your product or service, they think of you first. Next, you need to deliver information about your product and service to them, in such a way that gets their attention, and makes them raise their hand and say "Yes! I am interested in what you have to say." An effective marketing campaign almost eliminates the need for the salesperson because the prospect is actively responding, saying, "I want your product or service."

The good news is, with Direct Mail, you can effectively cover all of the marketing aspects covered in this book. If you work with a professional provider, this can be largely hands-off for you. Sure, there is some work in the beginning to create the campaigns. But once it's all set up, you can sit back and let your Direct Mail provider do the work, and let the mail deliver a steady stream of targeted prospects to your door.

Direct Mail really is Alive and Kickin'. Take advantage of it and watch your business grow to heights you never imagined possible.

If you would like some help with marketing your business, at any level, we can help. I own a *"One Stop Image Shop"* - Graphic Connections Group, and we specialize in helping clients develop complete marketing campaigns, with direct mail being a key element. The goal of every campaign is to provide increased profits to the business owner so you can experience all that life has to offer.

I welcome your call.

Jeff Charlton

9781631101465